LITERARY CONNECTICUT

LITERARY CONNECTICUT
The Hartford Wits, Mark Twain and the New Millennium

Eric D. Lehman and
Amy Nawrocki

THE
History
PRESS

Published by The History Press
Charleston, SC 29403
www.historypress.net

Cover images courtesy of the Library of Congress and Kris Nawrocki.

First published 2014

ISBN 9781540221919

Library of Congress CIP data applied for.

Contents

Preface

We often hear from discouraged English teachers that literature is dead and that no one reads anymore. Sometimes we are those English teachers. But with all due respect to us hardworking, front-line soldiers in the war for reading comprehension, we are wrong. Perhaps we are experiencing "golden age thinking," dreaming of some mystical past when everyone read poetry in their living rooms instead of watching television. It's sad to say that such a time never existed. Only the super-educated portion of the upper class experienced this literary life, and 99 percent of the population never participated. Now that education is nearly universal, we complain that not everyone wants to read Wallace Stevens's "Thirteen Ways of Looking at a Blackbird" aloud at dinner parties.

But guess what? Noah Webster's dictionary is one of the bestselling products of all time. People still stage *Our Town* all over the world. *Huckleberry Finn* continues to shine a light on the evils of racism and hypocrisy for every one of the hundreds of millions who have read it. That's right, hundreds of millions. Still discouraged? How about some statistics, like the fact that book sales keep rising and literacy rates keep growing around the world? And more people are writing, too. Thanks to the modern ease of self-publishing and e-texts, the number of published authors has increased a hundredfold. That doesn't sound like a culture in decline. As Connecticut's own Mark Twain put it so sarcastically, "Literature is well enough, as a time-passer, and for the improvement and general elevation and purification of mankind, but it has no practical value." No practical value, indeed.

The premier network of libraries across the state offers readers the chance to connect with the state's literary greats. The Pequot Library in Southport is one of the best. *Library of Congress.*

For those of us in Connecticut, the healthy condition of literature is more noticeable than in some places. Despite our small size, we have a surprising 183 public libraries, from the Mark Twain Library in Redding, donated by the great author himself, to the oldest free lender in the country, Scoville Memorial Library in Salisbury. Appropriately, our libraries are housed in some of the most beautiful buildings in the state, wonderful Romanesque masterpieces and modern glass-walled wonders. We are consistently rated one of the most educated states in America, with many advanced-degree earners, library visits per capita and colleges per citizen. We are readers.

And where you find readers, you will find writers. Whether in the rolling western hills, the ivy-clothed halls of our universities or along the rocky shore of Long Island Sound, writers have found their inspiration and passion here for centuries. You will encounter some of the most important figures in American literature here and some you have never heard of. Some were born here, some lived most of their lives here and some just passed through.

Some transformed poetry, and some created American language from the ground up. We have America's most famous novelist and America's first literary movement. An astonishing four of the five most respected dramatists of the twentieth century lived in Connecticut.

It is a rich trove for such a small, quiet state. But we plainly live in a place where culture is not just consumed but also created, where the ferment and fire take place inside, fingers poised over a quill pen or keyboard. We are lucky enough to send out that fire to the world and keep the quiet for ourselves. Creating literature is a human activity—we all do it, even if we are just telling a funny story about our uncle and a pig. But few people write those stories down, and even fewer are read by more than their families.

Bridgeport's Richard Osborn was an expatriate friend to *Tropic of Cancer* author Henry Miller, and the two corresponded afterward for many years. Osborn claimed to have completed a long novel about his years in Paris and to have collected Miller's letters and his own for publication. But he died, and his mysterious trunk of papers was destroyed by a high-minded brother-in-law, never to be read by anyone. Of course, what happened to Osborn is a tragedy. When any person dies and their mental warehouse of stories is lost, it is a tragedy. It leaves a hole in the world. That is why great writers are so important—their work stands in for all those lost tales; they tell our stories as if they knew us, as if they verbalized the unwritten longings of our souls.

In that way, great writers perform a sort of magic, taking everyday words and arranging them into spells, sometimes a few lines, sometimes hundreds of pages long, and when the spell is read, something changes inside the reader. If the spell is very good, the culture itself might change. Those are the writers who touch us, who transform us, who belong in books like this one. They are the magicians of Connecticut, giving strength or granting doubt, exploring darkness or bringing light.

Who are they, these magical beings? Surprisingly, they drove the same roads as we do today, frequented the same taverns, maybe even shopped at the same stores. They ate the same food and, yes, read the same books. They lived in our largest cities and smallest villages, along the rivers and on the farms, in small cabins and huge mansions, with large families or alone, like everyday ordinary people. It's time to get to know your neighbors.

Twilight of the Puritans

When Jonathan Edwards was one year old, French soldiers and their Indian allies raided down from Canada and attacked Deerfield, Massachusetts, upriver from his home in East Windsor, Connecticut. It was one of many attacks during Queen Anne's War, which lasted throughout his childhood. His father, Reverend Timothy Edwards, served as a chaplain on an expedition in 1711, but his health was not suited for military life, and he returned home early in some disgrace to his small village on the banks of New England's greatest river.

There in East Windsor, little Jonathan learned his Bible from his many sisters and his mother, Esther, a dignified yet gentle woman. His father, Timothy, was an affectionate disciplinarian who expected a lot from his children. His own mother, Jonathan's grandmother, was given to fits of violence and had cheated on his grandfather just after their marriage. In fact, that entire branch of the family had psychological issues: his great-aunt murdered her child, and his great-uncle murdered another sister with an axe.

Perhaps Timothy Edwards was atoning for his mother's family's sins as he preached revivals and awakenings throughout the area. In 1712 or 1713, at only nine years old, Jonathan himself felt "remarkable seasons of awakening" and came to a "new sense of things." He prayed in his room five times a day and organized prayer meetings with other children in East Windsor. It was the beginning of his life's work.

Jonathan grew into a tall, thin boy and, at age thirteen, left for Weathersfield to attend the Collegiate School, which had not settled into one permanent home yet. But by his third year of college, a gift from merchant Elihu Yale allowed a long, blue wooden building in New Haven to become the center of what would now be called Yale College. New Haven, the first planned city in the colonies, bustled with trade and commerce. The Yale students lived on the west side of the town green and came into contact with the world both through their books and through the shipping trade. Unfortunately, the latter also brought them into contact with various diseases. During his senior year, Edwards contracted pleurisy and nearly died. Though at first this event deepened his religious conviction, he "fell again into my old ways of sin," as we might expect from any normal sixteen-year-old.

Jonathan Edwards's seminal lecture "Sinner in the Hands of an Angry God" frightened the unrepentant into a renewal of faith. *From* A Library of American Literature, *1888. Magnus Wahlstrom Library, University of Bridgeport.*

The world Jonathan inhabited was one just beginning to peek out of the religious theocracy of the Puritan settlers. Sitting through a dozen hours of sermons a week was no longer for everyone, and many were now dissenting from the original dissenting positions of the Congregational churches. It was also a world in which women were just beginning to find their way out of the medieval constraints of patriarchy. Some were even writing their experiences and opinions down on paper.

One of those women was Sarah Knight, born about 1665 in Massachusetts. She might have been married, but no one knows for sure, though she did have a daughter named Elizabeth. In 1698, she appeared in the village of Norwich, Connecticut, telling people she was a widow and shopkeeper. She stayed there four years, selling her products beneath the rocky hillsides near Yantic Falls. She left the state but passed through again in 1704, recording her journey in one of America's first travelogues. Her prose vividly describes a frontier world full of charming characters and mundane troubles, as in this hilarious passage about a meal in eastern Connecticut:

> *Here, having called for something to eat, ye woman bro't in a Twisted thing like a cable, but something whiter; and laying it on the bord, tugg'd for life to bring it into a capacity to spread; which having with great pains accomplished, shee serv'd in a dish of Pork and Cabage, I suppose the remains of Dinner. The sause was of a deep Purple, which I tho't was boil'd in her dye Kettle; the bread was Indian, and every thing on the Table service agreeable to these. I, being hungry, gott a little down; but my stomach was soon cloy'd, and what cabbage I swallowed serv'd me for a Cudd the whole day after.*

By 1717, Knight had returned to Norwich, rich enough to donate a silver communion cup to the church. On August 12, 1717, she was allowed to "sit in the pew where she used to sit." However, she was clearly no saint. On March 26, 1718, she and six other people were indicted for "selling strong drink to the Indians." She pointed the finger at her maid, Ann Clark, but

Sarah Knight's journal, chronicling her travels on horseback from Boston to New York, provides a comical picture of colonial life. Her tavern in Norwich still exists as a private home. *Courtesy of the authors.*

was fined anyway. In 1724, she bought land on the road to the port town of New London, trying her hand at farming and innkeeping. She died there three years later, one of America's first female authors.

By this time, Jonathan Edwards had attended Yale for his master's degree, having "great and violent struggles" with his own spirituality, as well as struggling with his introversion and trouble relating to other students. He served as the college butler and became shocked by the petty thieving of most students, who took freely "hens, geese, turkeys, pigs, meat, and wood." Most students, including those training for the ministry, played cards, cursed and committed petty acts of vandalism—appalling the disciplined, intense Edwards. He often wandered alone in the farmlands and forests outside town, under the huge cliffs of East and West Rock and along the banks of the Quinnipiac River. In nature, he found "a kind of vision…being alone in the mountains, or some solitary wilderness, far from all mankind, swiftly conversing with Christ, and wrapped up and swallowed up in God."

After graduation and a short stint in New York City, his father tried to get him a position as pastor in nearby Bolton, a recently settled village on the edge of a wild range of hills. However, Edwards was more interested in writing by this point, combining his deep religious beliefs with contemporary philosophy and his interest in natural science. Like many in the eighteenth century, he worked to reconcile the burgeoning scientific discoveries of the day with a creator God who was involved in every aspect of it. He wrote on excellence, beauty and harmony, forming the basis for what would become the most impressive collection of sermons in the century.

Edwards did not last long in Bolton, and when offered a position as a tutor at Yale, he returned to New Haven. He continued to keep his diary and write sermons, really taut philosophical essays, and fell in love with a girl named Sarah Pierpont, daughter of one of the most important men in town. They sang duets together, and Edwards wrote: "Happiness. How soon earthly lovers come to an end of their discoveries of each other's beauty; how soon do they see all that is to be seen!" Even the love of his beautiful Sarah could not compete with the love of God. Nevertheless, they were married in 1727 in New Haven and the next year had a daughter. Edwards was offered an assistant ministry in Northampton, Massachusetts, with his grandfather Solomon Stoddard. The small family settled there, within a day's ride of his birthplace.

In Northampton, Edwards had fifty acres of land and a steady income, but he also had 1,300 people in his congregation. He rose every day at four or five o'clock in the morning and spent up to thirteen hours in his study, reading and writing. He began to suffer from anxiety, a malady that included losing his voice and "childish weakness." After his grandfather died, Edwards had to decide which was more important, making calls to his parishioners or using his gifts to write works of spiritual literature. He decided on the latter, and while Sarah managed the house and took care of their many children with the help of a female slave and farm laborers, Edwards wrote and wrote. Only while taking long horseback rides and chopping wood was he afforded time to contemplate eternity.

But his work bore fruit. The first Great Awakening began sweeping over New England in the early 1730s, especially in the Connecticut River Valley. Edwards was at the forefront of this revival of religious feeling as a preacher and as a writer. His book *A Faithful Narrative of the Surprising Work of God* became an inspiration for revivals in Scotland and England. By the time an American edition of the work was published in 1738, it was already a classic.

Some of his sermons had a tender tone, such as "Heaven Is a World of Love," but it was his hellfire and brimstone sermon "Sinners in the Hands of an Angry God" that became a sensation. Edwards tried a version of this sermon on his own congregation and revised it for his July 8, 1741 guest sermon at Enfield, Connecticut. The lecture produced amazing results. A contemporary, Samuel Hopkins of Waterbury, tells us that Edwards exhorted his listeners in vivid language, speaking "with such gravity and solemnity" and "with such distinctness, clearness and precision; his words were so full of ideas, set in such as plane [*sic*] and striking light, that few speakers have been so able to demand the attention of an audience as he." He exhorted them:

> *The God that holds you over the pit of hell, much as one holds a spider, or some loathsome insect over the fire, abhors you, and is dreadfully provoked: his wrath towards you burns like fire; he looks upon you as worthy of nothing else, but to be cast into the fire; he is of purer eyes than to bear to have you in his sight; you are ten thousand times more abominable in his eyes, than the most hateful venomous serpent is in ours. You have offended him infinitely more than ever a stubborn rebel did his prince; and yet it is nothing but his hand that holds you from falling into the fire every moment.*

He continued describing the horrible torments that awaited those without Christ. People moaned and shouted out from the pews, begging him to tell them what they needed to do to be saved. Witness Ola Winslow claimed that Edwards had to "desist" at points when the "shrieks and cries" became too "piercing." The winter before had been the hardest to hit New England since the arrival of the pilgrims, and the people were ready to hear about the hope of salvation.

Not everyone was happy with the "New Lights" of the Great Awakening, and these traditional folks became known as the "Old Lights." One was poet and businessman Roger Walcott. A generation older than Edwards, he was born just down the road in Windsor. With no formal schooling, he apprenticed at age twelve as a mechanic and rose steadily in reputation throughout the early years of the eighteenth century. His poetry was another matter, though his 1725 volume, *Poetical Meditations; Being the Improvement of Some Vacant Hours*, found contemporary success. It included a poem on how the colony acquired its charter from King Charles II and several religious themes that might have provided Edwards with some pause:

> *Oh what is man, that though shouldest allow*
> *Him to Inherit thy divine compassion?*
> *What is the sinful Son of man, that thou*
> *Should'st grant him thy Spirit's visitation?*
> *And suffer thine Eternal SON to dye,*
> *To Reconcile thy stubborn Enemy!*

Eventually, Walcott would serve as governor of Connecticut, and his son Oliver would also become the governor and one of the signers of the Declaration of Independence.

Edwards was tolerant of the Old Lights' friendly competition, though he continued to fight against hypocrites and egoists. In fact, he became more of a conservative reformer as the enthusiasm for religious revival began to wane throughout the 1740s. He fought to suppress the use of public profanity and what we would call sexual harassment, something that unfortunately did not endear him to the young people of western Massachusetts. His congregation became divided over various issues, and he moved west in 1751 to Stockbridge, where he hoped his traditionalist reforms would be better appreciated amongst the Indians who lived there. He found more strife and some success, though his writings became more and more popular around the world. His book *Freedom of the Will* influenced Calvinism in both Scotland and America, giving a deep philosophical background to its doctrine. He wrote on original sin, on the importance of community life, on the nature of virtue and on the question of why God created the world. And he worked on defining true love, which he posited was to make others happy without thought for oneself.

Seven years later, at age fifty-five, he moved to Princeton, New Jersey, to become a professor of divinity. Shortly after arriving in Princeton, he had his family inoculated for smallpox. But something went wrong, and while his family recovered, the roof of Edwards's mouth and throat filled with the small red marks of the deadly disease. His daughter Lucy had traveled with them, and he called her to his bedside, telling her, "It seems to me to be the will of God that I must shortly leave you; therefore give my kindest love to my dear wife, and tell her, that the uncommon union, which has so long subsisted between us, has been of such a nature, as I trust is spiritual, and therefore will continue forever."

Edwards had provided a model of spiritual energy and literary skill that inspired generations of ministers and preachers. Two of his local literary descendants were the Reverend John Pierpont and the Reverend Aaron Cleveland, both of whom combined poetic flair with religious zeal. Pierpont was from the family of Edwards's wife, born in Litchfield in 1785 and a graduate of Yale and the Tapping Reeve Law School in his hometown. His work in poetry first manifested in Massachusetts, where he "delivered" a patriotic poem entitled "The Portrait." After some publishing success, he

As the state's only eighteenth-century college, Yale University cultivated early literary greats from Jonathan Edwards to the Hartford Wits. Completed in 1753 to relieve overcrowding, Connecticut Hall is Yale's oldest remaining dormitory. *Library of Congress.*

turned his professional attention to studying theology, working for a Boston Unitarian church. He traveled to Europe and Asia Minor, and his best-known poem, "Airs of Palestine," is a good example of his careful verse, which varied bold and delicate rhythms.

Aaron Cleveland grew up an orphan in Haddam, Connecticut, and unlike Pierpont did not have the means for a college education. He studied poetry on his own while working in a factory in Norwich, and at age nineteen, he wrote "The Philosopher and Boy" and began to publish anonymously. He did not experience the church's call until late in life, when he became a pastor near Hartford known for "child-like tendencies of spirit" and his poetic wit, with which he urged his parishioners against too much "soberness." However, he could be serious, and his long poem "On Slavery," written in blank verse, expressed a very progressive view, not only of slavery, but also about the oppression of all people. His great-grandson Grover went on to become president of the United States.

Meanwhile, Jonathan Edwards's sermons and essays were printed and distributed by the hundreds of thousands, finding their way into the hands of many poor sinners, as well as more skeptical readers like Benjamin Franklin. Edwards became the first American minister with a truly international reputation, which showed no sign of diminishing as the centuries passed. In the twentieth century, his alma mater, Yale, named an entire college for him, and as their mascot, the students chose a lowly spider, wryly referencing Edwards's stern warning that each of us offensive, rebellious sinners dangles precariously over an eternal flame.

The Revolution of the Hartford Wits

W e often hear that war leads to great literature. But the War for Independence produced only one literary movement, usually called the Hartford or Connecticut Wits. Perhaps most of the gifted writers on the continent were too busy creating a new form of government. But in between battles and committee work, a few tried their hands at poetry. Joel Barlow, John Trumbull, Timothy Dwight, David Humphreys and their friends were all inspired by the Revolution to write the myths of the new nation. Somehow, though, when American literature courses are created, they usually skip directly from Jonathan Edwards to James Fenimore Cooper as if the years between were too full of bloodshed and struggle to produce authors. Removing the story of Connecticut's Wits might be good for contemporary aesthetic tastes, but it is bad as a matter of historical accuracy.

The oldest of the Wits was cousin to Connecticut's most famous family, the Trumbulls, who shepherded the state through the Revolution and into a new world. Born in 1750 in Watertown, little John Trumbull was a prodigy, passing a college entrance exam at age seven. Luckily, his preacher father held him back a few more years at least. When he finally entered Yale in 1763, at age thirteen, he had already mastered Greek, so he concentrated on mathematics and astronomy, later delving deeper into philosophy and metaphysics.

New Haven had grown since the time of Jonathan Edwards, and so had Yale, but it was still small compared to what it would become. Trumbull squeezed into the tiny rooms of Old College Hall's three-story dormitory with dozens of other students. Nearby, the newer Connecticut Hall and the chapel were the only other buildings on campus. Like college students of any time in history, they drank cider and wine and made do with what seemed poor dinner fare from the kitchens. The professors at Yale had very traditional ideas about learning and certainly didn't teach poetry writing or any of the other arts. Students had to learn them on their own or with friends.

Trumbull would find one of those friends two years after he matriculated. Originally from Northampton, Massachusetts, Timothy Dwight was the grandson of Jonathan Edwards. He arrived at Yale in 1765, at age thirteen, taking his uncle Jonathan Edwards Jr. as his mentor. In some ways, Dwight was Trumbull's opposite—healthy, strong, honey-voiced and eager to improve his mind. In fact, he was one of the most studious people his classmates ever saw, waking early enough to read one hundred lines of Homer before the chapel bells rang. But he wasn't always such a dedicated scholar. He arrived at Yale just in time to witness and participate in a small rebellion by all the students that led to a near dissolution of the college. This was also the year of the infamous Stamp Act riots throughout the colonies, and social disorder was the norm.

John Trumbull was the most popular American poet of his day, and like the other Wits, he used satire and political humor to underscore a deeply patriotic yet critical zeal for the new country. *From* A Library of American Literature, *1888. Magnus Wahlstrom Library, University of Bridgeport.*

Luckily, discipline returned to the college, and fewer students spent their weekends protesting, whether through vandalism or satirical letters. Dwight's personal discipline grew to legendary proportions; he rigidly controlled his food intake, eventually becoming a vegetarian, an experiment that gave him attacks of "bilious colic" and reduced him to "nearly a skeleton." At death's door, Dwight recovered when a doctor gave him a program of long walks and horse riding. However, several years later he was inoculated for smallpox, and this, combined with over-studying, led to eye damage. He put on thick, horn-rimmed glasses and soldiered on. At least the inoculation had not killed him, as it had his grandfather Edwards.

Trumbull and Dwight began studying literature on their own, since college was for learning long-dead languages, not contemporary sciences and humanities. The Yale Library did have the best collection of eighteenth-century literature in New England, and whatever cutting-edge books were missing, students could find down the street at Benedict Arnold's bookstore. Along with reading outside the curriculum, Trumbull and Dwight broke other rules. Against college doctrine, they acted in plays at private houses and took part in secret literary societies. Some of what the college proffered, they took eagerly, and some they rejected wholeheartedly. But their experience at school primarily made them think and apply their pens to the questions of the day.

They were joined by another bright boy named David Humphreys, who had grown up in Derby as the youngest of five children. He loved books, and a college education seemed like the only way to satisfy this love. Though the same age as Dwight, Humphreys entered Yale two years later, in 1767, at the ripe old age of fifteen. The promising scholar fit right into their secret literary society and became a supporter of their worldview. Trumbull's oration at commencement, "An Essay on the Use and Advantages of the Fine Arts," included hearty criticism of the eighteenth-century style of education and a plea for introducing the arts into college life. But the friends did not reject Yale entirely. In fact, Trumbull, Dwight and Humphreys all became college tutors, and Dwight befriended a promising young student named Nathan Hale.

The first major publication of any of the Wits came from Trumbull, who expanded on the theme of his commencement speech in a long poem called "The Progress of Dulness [sic]." It was a send-up of the foibles of college education, including the adventures of students "Tom Brainless," "Dick Hairbrain" and "Harriet Simper." Their experiences seem fairly universal, and most students or teachers today can relate:

Four years of college dozed away
In sleep, in slothfulness and play,
Too dull for vice, with clearest conscience
Charged with no fault but that of nonsense,
And nonsense long, with serious air
Has wandered long unmolested there,
He passes trial, fair and free,
And takes in form his first degree.

After "Dulness" was finished, Trumbull took a break from Yale to work in the offices of a Boston lawyer named John Adams, but the upheavals following the Boston Tea Party drove him back to New Haven.

Three years later, a boy named Joel Barlow transferred from Dartmouth. Barlow came from a poor farming family in Redding and went to private school and Dartmouth on what we would call financial aid. At Yale, he polished a few bad habits and, as a tall, good-looking young man, easily made lots of friends, including the growing band of literary lions under Trumbull, Dwight and Humphreys. All were in love with the idea of progress, though all had different ideas of what that might mean. Barlow wrote to his classmate Noah Webster, "Let us show the world a few more examples of men standing upon their own merit, and rising in spite of opposition."

But Barlow's transfer to Yale came just before the whirlwind. Students voted to stop drinking tea, and during the spring semester of 1775, the Battle of Lexington sparked the American Revolution. Barlow

In addition to poetry, Joel Barlow dabbled in law, politics and diplomacy, trying to advance the fortunes of his new nation. *From* A Library of American Literature, *1888. Magnus Wahlstrom Library, University of Bridgeport.*

and Humphreys left New Haven to serve in the Continental army, and in 1777, Dwight gave up his position as teacher at the college to become an army chaplain. Humphreys left his tutoring job and, on his departure for the army, wrote a sonnet to his friends. Almost everyone they knew was involved in the Revolution in one way or another. Many of their college friends became officers, and some died. Nathan Hale, remembering his Yale literary club days before he was hanged as a spy, paraphrased Addison's play *Cato*, saying, "I only regret I have but one life to lose for my country."

Only John Trumbull did not serve in the army but gave his own contribution to the war effort with *M'Fingal*, a mock epic with many satiric jabs at Loyalists: "True to their King, with firm devotion, / For Conscience sake and hop'd promotion." The caricatures of people like British general William Howe appealed to many, but Trumbull's genius lay in bringing the entire war down to human size and setting the argument at a typical New England town meeting, something to which every one of his readers could relate. The climax comes when Loyalist Squire M'Fingal is defeated and hoisted by his middle up the liberty pole, to hang there until he swears allegiance to America. He breaks immediately, but after the townspeople put him on trial, he flees, leaving everyone disappointed that they could not punish him further. However, because the squire has so much voice in the epic, later readers would note that Trumbull did not leave the too eager and violent Patriots off scot-free, and the balanced satire of human politics became the only Revolutionary-era poem to last long beyond the war.

The others continued to write throughout their service in the army. David Humphreys moved steadily up the ranks, eventually becoming a colonel directly under George Washington. In 1780, he wrote—as he said, "instigated by the Devil and a certain Jere[miah] Wadsworth"—a poem to inspire soldiers called "Address to the Armies" and an elegy on the burning of Fairfield by the British. "Address" was a big hit and later sold many copies in England and the United States. His next poem, on the "happiness" of America, was also a success. Joel Barlow began a longer epic poem, using Christopher Columbus as the hero, and while planning and writing this, he continually wrote other shorter rhymes. On October 17, 1780, he and Humphreys dined with George Washington, no doubt discussing the infamous treachery of Benedict Arnold, who had been stopped just in time, partly through the quick thinking of their classmate Benjamin Tallmadge. Having recently become a minister, Barlow also gave a sermon that autumn on "The Treasons of Arnold and the Glory of America." A year later, the war was effectively over, and Humphreys himself presented Cornwallis's surrendered banner to the Continental Congress.

Joel Barlow secretly married Ruth Baldwin in 1781 and, after the war, settled in Hartford, taking the jobs of editor, storekeeper and lawyer. Trumbull had moved there in 1780, and now Barlow began to adopt his older friend's easier style of writing. His larger work *The Vision of Columbus* was finally finished in March of that year, but it was a thin effort that did not have either philosophical weight or considerable wit. Whatever its faults, it connected Columbus with Anglo-American experience in a way that would shape future national mythology for two hundred years. The other Wits helped him finish it, and it finally went to press in 1786. A huge list of subscribers from the upper ranks of the army made its first printing a success, but subsequent printings were less than profitable. Clearly, there was little money to be gained in the pursuit of poetry.

At the end of the war in 1783, Timothy Dwight accepted the pastorate in Greenfield, now part of Fairfield, and settled there. His interest in the literary aspect of the Bible led him to defend it on the grounds of its compositional genius rather than its moralistic merits. At the age of nineteen, he began an epic in heroic couplets that he eventually called *The Conquest of Canaan*, a story that interestingly deviated from "biblical authority" and included well-drawn characters, like the Old Testament's Joshua, portrayed in a much better light than in the Bible. In fact, the characters were a fascinating combination of modern Americans, ancient Greeks and Hebrew heroes. Dwight was following a common belief at the time: the connection between the Israelites and the Americans, something deeply ingrained in Connecticut lore. He also added a romantic love story to the epic, something that certainly didn't hurt its interest for the masses. Like many in the eighteenth century, though, he was much more interested in the meaning of the poetry than in its sound or audience appeal.

The rest of the group gathered in one place. One of Barlow's old friends, Dr. Lemuel Hopkins of Litchfield, joined him in Hartford in 1784, and they collaborated with John Trumbull to revise the Christian Psalm book to reflect the new America, removing mentions of king and England. Middletown's Richard Alsop was keeping a bookstore in Hartford and joined the group as well. By the time David Humphreys returned from negotiating treaties in Europe to serve in the state legislature, a full-fledged literary movement had been born. They also met frequently to discuss politics and philosophy and published in the new nation's literary journals, at this time first becoming known as the Wits. The word implies to modern ears that they were comedy writers, and while occasionally their poetry tickled the funny bone, they were, in fact, very serious about their endeavors.

However, Barlow and the others had goals that went beyond art. All were interested in serving the new republic they had helped create. Both Trumbull and Barlow were elected to the Common Council of Hartford in March 1786. The state was dealing with the economic repercussions of the Revolution, a small civil war in Pennsylvania over claims to the upper Susquehanna Valley and the possibility of a new colony on the shores of Lake Erie. The Revolution was over, and the difficult work of governing had begun. Politics had already begun to divide the previously united Revolutionaries, and opinions on these and other subjects of the day began to appear in the newspapers with increasing venom.

The Wits began to get involved, collaborating on a long satire called *Anarchiad: A Poem on the Restoration of Chaos and Substantial Night.* They were worried that the new obsession with individual freedom would lead to a breakdown of society in which "every rogue shall literally do what is right in his own eyes." And where would this lead? Back to tyranny as it so often does. From the heights of proclaiming national revolution, the Wits had been drawn into mere politics. Of course, they did not see it that way—they were fighting for the soul of the new nation. Unfortunately, almost all literature based on politics becomes of the moment rather than immortal, personal rather than universal. They also misjudged many of the Connecticut representatives whom they specifically targeted in the *Anarchiad*, all of whom voted to ratify the new federal Constitution.

Timothy Dwight contributed to the *Anarchiad*, even though as a practicing minister he was supposed to be above that. He had a lot of other duties, too: running a farm, writing for newspapers and teaching at Greenfield Academy. One of his students, Elihu Hubbard Smith, became a doctor but, after moving to Wethersfield, embraced the literary life, joining the older generation of Wits. Along with writing his own poetic operas, Smith edited *American Poems, Selected and Original*, published in 1793 in Litchfield, which included poems by Trumbull, Dwight, Barlow, Humphreys, Hopkins, Alsop and others. It was the first general collection of poetry ever attempted in America.

Dwight continued preaching sermons at his Greenfield church, alternately quarrelsome and contented. At one point, he poetically attacked the idea that perfection was possible and that each political fight was an endgame:

> *Slow, by degrees, politic systems rise;*
> *Age still refines them, and experience tries.*

This, this alone consolidates, improves;
Their sinews strengthens; their defects removes.

But he was more and more turning his pen to theology, something that also was not without controversy. In fact, his long work *The Triumph of Infidelity* caused a fight with the pastor of First Church of Boston. Many who had admired Dwight were stunned by the "malevolence" of his pen in the arguments that raged, and even his friend Noah Webster thought the work bad, not because of its theological precepts but because of a lack of honest character.

At the same time, David Humphreys turned from poetry to history. While talking with the old warhorse General Israel Putnam, he decided to write Putnam's biography, and though the attempt ended more in patriotic mythology than true history, he contributed to the classic stories like Putnam crawling into the wolf den alone and riding down the steps in Greenwich to escape the British. These stories might have had their origin in truth, but written down, they had more in common with a young George Washington chopping down a cherry tree. The biography, however, was a

David Humphreys's seventeenth-century house is the only remaining home of the Wits. Better known as General Washington's aide de camp, Humphreys appears next to the future president in the painting *Washington Resigning His Position* in the Capitol Rotunda. *Courtesy of the Derby Historical Society.*

huge success, and Humphreys worked on one of Washington himself based on his conversations with the great man. Then, in 1790, Humphreys left the group for Europe as a "special secret agent" for Washington's presidential administration, a position he kept in one way or another until the Federalist Party left power in 1801.

Barlow also headed abroad, sailing for France as a member of the Ohio Company, a business concern that promptly failed. Undamaged by this and beloved by the French, the thirty-two-year-old poet became a citizen in the winter of 1791–92, just before things there went downhill. He survived the Terror and, through various shady business ventures, earned enough money to stop working by 1796, becoming the minister to Algiers along the way. Somehow he stayed on the good side of the changing and violent French government. In Paris in 1797, he began supporting promising young men like Robert Fulton, developer of the first commercial steamboat. Barlow also traveled to England, Africa and Germany, meeting Tom Paine and Mary Wollstonecraft. He continued to write about his belief in progress, especially the idea that education and political development could improve character. "Banish the mysticism of inequality and you banish almost all the evil attendant on human nature," he wrote. He began to feel homesick for America, and not just for democracy. At a smoky Savoyard inn, he ate a dish of hasty pudding, under the name polenta, and wrote the hilarious three-canto poem for which he is best remembered, regaling the virtues of this classic New England dish:

> *My father loved thee through his length of days;*
> *For thee his fields were shaded o'er with maize;*
> *From thee what health, what vigor he possessed,*
> *Ten sturdy freemen from his loins attest;*
> *Thy constellation ruled my natal morn,*
> *And all my bones were made of Indian corn.*

Meanwhile, back in Connecticut, probably satisfied by many dishes of hasty pudding, Timothy Dwight pulled himself back from his theologically aggressive brink, writing *Greenfield Hill*, an amiable celebration of the local scene and of American virtues. He wrote that facts and real life would cause men to "politic wisdom learn"—and perhaps this was an admonition to his own sometimes impolitic nature.

After *Greenfield*, Dwight turned more and more to prose, writing sermons like "The Dignity and Excellence of the Gospel" and "The True Means of

Establishing Public Happiness." By 1795, he had been tapped to become the next president of Yale. He had come a long way since writing angry college boy screeds in the New Haven papers. Now he could create policy and move Yale into the future he imagined. He promoted Locke's *Essay Concerning the Human Understanding* as a keystone for all students and began the slow process away from ancient languages to the arts and sciences of a modern university.

In 1800, John Trumbull was elected to a judgeship and stopped writing political poetry, saying that he refused "any interference in the politics of the state...being of the opinion that the character of a partisan and political writer was inconsistent with the station of a judge." It does not seem to have occurred to him that there might be other subjects worthy of his pen. In fact, a new type of poetry was coming out of England at this time, but Trumbull had no use for William Wordsworth's "Romantic" *Lyrical Ballads*. Trumbull continued to act as judge of the Connecticut Superior Court and Supreme Court of Errors for the next two decades, turning as so many of his generation did to public service.

Joel Barlow's wife's health was failing, and they feared crossing the Atlantic too many more times; thus, they decided to return to America once and for all. He was also disappointed that the French Revolution had descended into a dictatorship. So in 1804, he left France, and he and his wife built a home in the new capital city of Washington, on a hill above Rock Creek called Kalorama, and filled it with paintings, wine and books. While there, he tried to found a national university based on combined research and instruction, a strange and radical idea at the time. He became more of a scholar than poet, researching mythology and language. He did revise his earlier work into *The Columbiad: A Vision of International Peace*, a longer and more philosophic version, writing:

> *Man is an infant still, and slow and late*
> *Must form and fix his adolescent state,*
> *Mature his manhood, and at last behold*
> *His reason ripen and his force unfold.*

It was published on Christmas Eve 1807, one of many poems that a hopeful Barlow thought could "do good" and propagate faith in democracy.

Finally, President Madison convinced the retired Barlow to become a minister to Napoleon, and he left for Europe again. Unfortunately, it was 1812, and trying to find the Corsican general, he reached Vilna, Russia, to wait for news of the retreat from Moscow. It was thirteen degrees below zero, and Napoleon passed Barlow in the night, fleeing possible assassination by his own troops. An ill Barlow followed to Warsaw and finally reached the town of Zarnowiec, where his friends made him stop and wait for medical assistance. But he died there, his last poem a bitter attack on the military dictator whom he believed had ruined France and the world.

Despite Timothy Dwight's poor eyesight and many duties as president of Yale, he took a second job as professor of theology. For twenty-two years, he guided classes of students toward graduation. His political and theological enemies attacked him frequently, but he had learned to rise above them. His literary output other than sermons diminished, but he did complete a work of travel literature, *Travels in New England and New York*, writing of the coast of Fairfield County, "There is not a more delightful spot of ground." Near the end of his life, he preached against the "love of distinction" that had driven him as a younger man. His theological doctrines mellowed, and he urged the unification of Congregationalists and Presbyterians, as well as making peace with Episcopalians.

David Humphreys and his wife had both liked the cosmopolitan life of Europe so much that they made their home in metropolitan Boston when they returned to America in 1801. However, Humphreys still visited Hartford and introduced Spanish merino sheep to Connecticut, building a successful woolen mill near Derby. He also dabbled in playwriting, producing *The Yankey in England*. It might not have been the best play, but it first codified the "Yankee" character for many people, a type that would dominate American literature until the cowboy replaced it sixty years later. He also spent some energy interested in a one-

Timothy Dwight started his writing career as a dissenting troublemaker at Yale College and ended it as its president. *From* A Library of American Literature, *1888. Magnus Wahlstrom Library, University of Bridgeport.*

hundred-foot sea serpent haunting the coast of New England, a phenomenon covered in all the newspapers. It was his last writing, and he died in 1818, leaving John Trumbull as the sole remaining figure from the old gang.

Though Trumbull had long since stopped writing poetry, the literary world had not forgotten the author of *M'Fingal*. In 1824, the nation's second literary movement, New York's Knickerbocker Club, gathered at a dinner to honor Trumbull. James Fenimore Cooper and Fitz-Greene Halleck raised their glasses to the aging veteran of American poetry, now in his seventy-fourth year. It was his last hurrah. Trumbull left Hartford a year later to live in Detroit with his daughter and son-in-law, the governor of Michigan. For six more years, he lived there, out of touch with his age and his own poetic muse, dying in 1831, the last and longest-lived of the Wits.

As the years went by, Trumbull and his cohorts fell out of favor with academics and the public alike. One "error of taste" is that they believed the American Revolution would herald a golden age of humanity, so their enthusiasm became too cloying for readers of more cynical times. The only exception was *M'Fingal* because the sarcasm and even-handedness of Trumbull's treatment prevented too much exaggeration. But satire does not wear well historically, either, and long poetry itself has lost its readership in the last century.

The Wits were failures in other ways, too. Their poetry failed to truly define the age or criticize it properly, failed to reach the heights of achievement of contemporary British poets and failed to trigger an American renaissance that would have to wait for future generations. They also failed to dedicate themselves solely to literature, as so many of the greatest writers have done. Dwight always said that he refused to live in a musty attic in order to become an author, and this was true of all of his generation. For better or worse, their true allegiance was to life, to serving the community and to their own ambitions rather than to the muse.

Nevertheless, as the new country's first literary movement, they demonstrated clearly that Americans would find their own voices and create their own literature. All focused introspectively on the concern of their age: the promise and danger of democracy, a topic that would continue to be the focus of popular culture for the next two centuries. Like many pioneers, they encountered difficulties, some of their own making, but others would follow the trembling path they carved through the dense forests of early America, clearing the brush so that today we can walk a broad and level highway.

Defining America

The youngest of the Hartford Wits was not a poet. In fact, he did not even write literature in the traditional sense. But what he wrote would change American literature and culture more dramatically and totally than the wildest dreams of his friends John Trumbull and Joel Barlow. While they were struggling to light the fuse of American poetry, their twenty-four-year-old friend Noah Webster became a bestselling writer. The book was actually a spelling textbook for schoolchildren, but it would become the most popular one of the next century. And there was more to come.

Born in 1758 in West Hartford, Webster was baptized by the great-great-grandson of Connecticut's founder, Thomas Hooker. The red-haired, gray-eyed child worked on the family farm, although more often he would be caught reading books under one of his father's apple trees. Attending primary school down the road, he found himself terrified and bored in turn. It might have been his frustration with his completely ineffective education that led to the quest of his lifetime. Less generous historians attribute it to narcissism—many described him as vain, stubborn and even spiteful. He was certainly obsessive-compulsive and full of opinions; at age twelve, he wrote an aggrieved letter to the editor of the *Connecticut Courant*, his first publication.

Only three years later, the tall, thin Webster enrolled at Yale. It was an auspicious time to be a college student; the year was 1774, and the first Continental Congress was meeting in Philadelphia. Furthermore, his best friend at Yale happened to be Joel Barlow, who introduced him to the literary

In his childhood home in West Hartford, Noah Webster learned his ABCs, often dodging work on his father's farm to read and write. He would incorporate what he learned into his "Blue-Backed Speller," the most popular book in early America, selling fifteen million copies before his death. *Courtesy of the authors.*

circles of the future Hartford Wits. Of course, he was also introduced into bad habits like swearing and spending time with attractive young women. When the war began, Webster and a huge crowd of Yale students escorted George Washington through New Haven as he rode to take command. In later years, Webster remembered fondly playing "Yankee Doodle Dandy" on his flute as the future president rode by.

Despite constant interruption from typhoid epidemics and fear of British attacks, Webster graduated, focusing on philosophy rather than poetry. Like many modern philosophy majors, he found himself struggling to find a job after graduation. However, in 1779, Webster moved in with and became an assistant to Oliver Ellsworth, future chief justice of the Supreme Court. He taught students at a nearby Hartford private school and in the evening helped Ellsworth's cases. However, this two-job schedule was too demanding, and he was forced to quit, returning to his father's farm to recover. He continued to dabble in law, trying to pass the bar, and moved to Litchfield, where he attended classes with Tapping Reeve at what became America's first law school. He continued to move around in the Litchfield Hills, living in Sharon and Goshen, working as a tutor and getting involved in a troubled love affair.

About this time in 1782, as the British planned their exit from the war, Webster began revising the Reverend Thomas Dilworth's famous spelling book, finding the English place names "totally useless." After fiddling with several titles, he decided on the *American Spelling Book*, though for the next four decades everyone knew it as the "Blue-Backed Speller" for its unique cover. He tried to regularize pronunciation and replace British references with purely American ones. Along with rules and regulations, he included proverbs, quotes from the Bible and fables from Aesop, like this disturbing one:

> *A fox, swimming across a river, happened to be entangled in some weeds that grew near the bank, from which he was unable to extricate himself. As he lay thus exposed to whole swarms of flies who were galling him, and sucking his blood, a swallow observing his distress, kindly offered to drive them away. By no means, said the Fox, for if these should be chased away, who are already sufficiently gorged, another more hungry swarm would succeed, and I should be robbed of every remaining drop of blood in my veins.*

Webster moved in with John Trumbull in Hartford and oversaw the speller's publication. An impressive list of Connecticut worthies endorsed it in the *Courant*. Overly excited, Webster became his own worst enemy, making grandiose and inflammatory statements in the press. His partisan tone on education turned off even his best supporters, and his critics attacked him for arrogance. However, as Connecticut showman P.T. Barnum would discover a few decades later, there was no such thing as bad publicity: the spelling books sold like hotcakes.

Finished with the spelling book, Webster next turned to political writing, making appeals for national unity and ranting at his enemies in turn. Even at this early date, he knew there was usually little to be gained by this sort of fleeting political prose. But he couldn't help himself and believed in the American project so firmly that he often took up his pen, sometimes anonymously, over the next several decades. One of his political efforts would in fact bear important fruit: he put his writing skills in the service of designing a stronger federal government and urging people to vote for the Constitution that created it. On May 20, 1785, he rode to Mount Vernon, where he met with his hero George Washington and tried to convince him that the Articles of Confederation were a joke and that the thirteen states needed a stronger connection between them. "We ought not to consider ourselves as inhabitants of a particular state only, but as Americans," he told Washington, who after his troubles with Congress and local governments during the war needed no convincing. Eventually, Webster's writing helped leaders like James Madison and Alexander Hamilton sell their vision of America to the people.

Throughout 1785 and 1786, Webster traveled across the country, using his obsessive-compulsive tendencies to count every house in the major towns he passed through. He gave lectures and sold books on one of the new nation's first author tours. In Philadelphia, he met Benjamin Franklin, and they discussed a mutual pet project, a plan to reform the English alphabet that was never put into practice. Webster witnessed fellow Connecticut inventor John Fitch sail the world's first steamboat on the Schuylkill River, and he was also in Philadelphia for an even more important event: the signing of the Constitution on September 17, 1787.

That same year, he met Rebecca Greenleaf, and they began seeing each other at teas and concerts. Webster fell head over heels in love, trying to shove down his arrogance and belligerence to woo Rebecca, who was from a proper Boston family. He told her that her friendship "is now my only happiness, and your happiness the great object of my pursuit," and that when he saw other ladies "there is not a Becca Greenleaf among them: no such tenderness, such delicacy, such sentiment, such unaffected goodness."

Webster moved back to Hartford, rooming with John Trumbull once again and even staying at former employer Oliver Ellsworth's house. Then, in the autumn of 1789, he married Rebecca, coming down with the flu on their honeymoon and bringing her back to Hartford, where they stayed in Jeremiah Wadsworth's mansion. Webster took up his pen again, arguing to pave the streets of the capital city with stone and for his perennial cause of spelling reform. He became an abolitionist in 1791, writing a fifty-page treatise called "Effects of Slavery on Morals and Industry." However, he needed to find a profession that would provide enough money to support his pretty, young wife and future family.

He went to work as an editor of the first New York daily newspaper, often financially helped by his wife's family. In 1796, he produced a book on yellow fever, a subject about which he knew absolutely nothing. He fell out with his old friend Joel Barlow in 1798, when he upbraided him for taking the part of the French against America. "As I know your character better than many of my countrymen, I am better entitled to comment freely on your opinions…it becomes you to speak of yourself with modesty and of your native country inner councils with more moderation and respect." Webster might have been correct in his assessment of the tyranny that the French Revolution had led to, but his need to argue ruined their friendship.

That same year, he moved to New Haven, to 155 Water Street, into the former home of American villain Benedict Arnold. It was a large two-story house with a stable, a garden and an orchard of peach and cherry trees. That year, he spoke at New Haven's Independence Day celebration, invited by former Wit Timothy Dwight, who was now the president of Yale. The invitation showed that Webster was already considered one of the state's most important citizens. But his greatest accomplishment was yet to come.

In the house on Water Street, he began a project that would take him almost three decades: a dictionary of the American language. We might think that this was a popular enterprise, seeing as the country had been free of England for almost two decades, but he was widely mocked and belittled. Less than a year later, his uncle asked him if he had finished yet, one of the first to vastly underestimate the job Webster had taken upon himself. In 1806, he published a short version, almost like a modern thesaurus, with forty thousand words, which Webster happily found Timothy Dwight was "much pleased with" and John Trumbull, the "best critic of this age," said would "stand its ground." This was the appetizer to the meal Webster was preparing for the American people.

His rich food of words would also have a nourishing effect on American literature, but in the meantime, things must have felt starved in Connecticut. A void had been left by the departure of the Hartford Wits from the scene, though some members of the new generation of writers were relatives of the originals. Richard Alsop's cousin John was born in 1776 and studied at Greenfield Hill Academy with Timothy Dwight before working under Tapping Reeve in Litchfield. He practiced law in New London, owned a bookstore in Hartford and, amongst his friends, was noted as a writer "distinguished by a graceful hilarity and humorous turn of thought." Theodore Dwight, related to both Timothy Dwight and John Alsop, wrote poetry, travel literature and *The History of Connecticut*. Others were sons of Revolutionary heroes, like the son of Norwich's General Jedediah Huntington, Daniel, who taught in New London at a girls' school and wrote religious poetry with "purity of sentiment."

Not everyone was a legacy, though. Selleck Osborn of Trumbull was born to a poor family the year the war ended, and his "delicate constitution" prohibited him from taking part in typical youthful activities, leading him to find comfort and knowledge in literature. He wrote political poetry of the style of the Wits, served in the War of 1812 and published a collected works in 1823. John Brainard of New London practiced law in Middletown, edited the *Connecticut Mirror* and wrote poetry, like "To the Connecticut River," where "the otter dives, the beaver feeds…the wild-cat purrs amid her brood." Near Noah Webster's house in New Haven, a young man named James Fenimore Cooper was attending Yale, playing pranks and getting in a lot of trouble. In fact, Yale "asked" him to leave in 1805, and he never graduated. But he did go on to become the bestselling novelist of the early 1800s, with classics like *The Spy* and *The Last of the Mohicans*.

James Abraham Hillhouse, born to a prominent New Haven family in 1789, graduated from Yale in 1808 with a master of arts degree. He worked in the mercantile business and pursued his art, producing verses like "Education of a Poet" and plays like *Percy's Masque, Drama in Five Acts*. Samuel Griswold Goodrich of Ridgefield became a bookseller, penning several volumes of his own under the pseudonym Peter Parley. His poem "Memory of Home" recounts:

> *I loved those hills, I loved the flowers*
> *That dashed with gems their sunny swells,*
> *And oft I fondly dreamed for hours,*
> *By streams within those mountain dells.*

Poets Edward McLaughlin of Bridgeport and George Hill of Guilford traveled the world, and the latter became librarian to the State Department in Washington, writing travel poems like "The Ruins of Athens." Joseph Nichols of Newtown stayed closer to home, studying at the Episcopal Academy of Cheshire, working at law in Litchfield and serving as minister in Greenwich, all while writing sentimental poems like "A Connecticut Christmas Eve." Some left the state forever, like Hebron's Hugh Peters, who left for Ohio to practice law. On the shores of Long Island Sound, he wrote his farewell to Connecticut:

> *The boat swings from the pebbled shore,*
> *And proudly drives her prow;*
> *The crested waves roll up before,*
> *Yon dark gray land I see no more,*
> *How sweet thou seemest now!*

Fitz-Greene Halleck of Guilford became part of the Knickerbocker Club, which followed the Hartford Wits as America's second literary movement. He found fans across the new nation, including a young Abraham Lincoln. *From* A Library of American Literature, *1888. Magnus Wahlstrom Library, University of Bridgeport.*

A few years later, he drowned in the Ohio River while sleepwalking, another poetic career failed of its promise.

However, two Connecticut poets would become America's most popular. Born and raised in Guilford, Fitz-Greene Halleck moved to New York and became a member of the new nation's second, and more successful, literary movement, the Knickerbocker Group, along with James Fenimore Cooper and Washington Irving. But he often wrote of his native state, saying:

> *'Tis a rough land of earth, and stone, and tree,*
> *Where breathes no castled lord or cabined slave;*
> *Where thoughts, and tongues, and hands, are bold and free,*
> *And friends will find a welcome, foes a grave;*
> *And where none kneel, save when to Heaven they pray,*
> *Nor even then, unless in their own way.*

Abraham Lincoln became a fan of Halleck and read his poetry aloud at the White House. After his death, Halleck was buried in Guilford, and a memorial was raised—the first in America to commemorate a poet.

Norwich native Lydia Sigourney was even more beloved. Born in 1791, she first established herself by developing and teaching at two academies for young girls, beginning in her hometown. Then, in 1814, she opened and operated a school in the home of Daniel Wadsworth, a prominent Hartford philanthropist. After marrying merchant Charles Sigourney in 1819, she began to write poetry in her leisure time, issuing a few works anonymously. Soon, however, rumors circulated, and she admitted to authorship of the conduct manual *Letters to Young Ladies, By a Lady*, henceforth publishing work under her own name.

Throughout her life, Sigourney remained committed to women in education and promoting religion and morality, with subjects that pushed her readers to understand the greater good of humanity across cultural and class boundaries. In the preface to her 1849 collection, *Illustrated Poems*, she invited readers in with these words:

> *In the alcove of the library, on the centre-table of the matron, to the ear of the young and beautiful, it shall breathe only pure thoughts, like the dew-drops lingering upon the rose. May it be found worthy to touch some chord of that spirit intercourse, to be perfected in a clime where the rose never fades, and the music-strain is immortal.*

During her lifetime, the "Sweet Singer of Hartford" was enormously popular, so much so that schoolchildren chanted her poem as the Revolutionary hero Marquis de Lafayette rode through town in 1824. While traveling in England, she dined with esteemed writers like William Wordsworth and Thomas Carlyle.

Though sometimes overly sentimental, Sigourney's verses are simple and accessible, integrating a love of words and ideas with useful moral guidelines and interesting constructs, memorializing the people, places and values of her time. She wrote elegies for close friends and memorials for public figures, lyrics about domestic childrearing, paeans to the beauty of nature and treatises on history, slavery and the plight of Native Americans. An advocate for the public will and community building, she reflected, "Still it is as useful and vastly more convenient, to admire objects near at hand than those far away." "The Butterfly" captures some of her themes and typical sentimentality:

> *A butterfly basked on a baby's grave,*
> *Where a lily had chanced to grow:*
> *"Why are thou here, with thy gaudy dye,*
> *When she of the blue and sparkling eye,*
> *Must sleep in the churchyard low?"*

Then it lightly soared through the sunny air,
And spoke from its shining track:
"I was a worm till I won my wings,
And she whom thou mourn'st like a seraph sings:
Wouldst thou call the blessed one back?"

Not everyone loved her poetry. Edgar Allan Poe roundly criticized her verse as derivative, though he later had to eat crow as the editor of a magazine that wanted her verse. In fact, the magazines of the day competed to feature her exclusively, and most critics praised her poetry, calling her "a poetess of the first rank." "Language is slow," she wrote in "Unspoken Language," a poem that takes the reader from the first words spoken to all the "deep eloquence" of the most intimate conversations. But Lydia Sigourney herself was certainly not slow, producing children's books and educational primers, memoirs that fused history and travel and over three hundred newspaper articles, as well as multiple poetry collections.

While Connecticut poetry experienced its second blossoming, Noah Webster ground away at the huge project that had become his life. But some things were going well for him. His family was growing, and in 1807, almost a decade after they had stopped speaking to each other, old friends Webster and Barlow made peace when the poet gave a favorable opinion on the idea of an expanded, comprehensive dictionary. Webster wrote to him kindly, saying, "You will recollect that Judge Trumbull and yourself for the only friends who in 1783 ventured to encourage me to publish my

"The Sweet Singer of Hartford" Lydia Sigourney achieved incredible popularity during her lifetime, helping to establish women as part of the American poetic canon. *Photo by Matthew Brady. Library of Congress.*

spelling book." Barlow in turn promised to send him a copy of his revised version of *The Columbiad*, and they renewed their correspondence before the poet's tragic death on Napoleon's retreat from Moscow.

The same year Barlow died, Webster sold Benedict Arnold's house and moved to Amherst, Massachusetts, where he continued to add to the gigantic tome. The income from his now bestselling spelling book was enough to keep his growing family satisfied, even though the royalty was less than one cent per copy. But eventually, Amherst was too small for Webster, lacking both the books and fellow scholars he needed to help him finish the dictionary. He moved back to New Haven into a custom-designed house on Temple Street. He continued slaving away in relative obscurity and finally finished, at age seventy, on November 26, 1828. And though his project had been scoffed at when he began, now that he was finished, everyone—both high and low—could see the worth of what he had done. His work changed spellings from English to American versions (such as centre to center and colour to color). And his definitions were clear and readable, with a few ironic exceptions, like "define," to which, understandably, he paid some extra attention:

> DEFINE, *verb transitive [Latin: To end, to limit, from finis, end.]*
> 1. *To determine or describe the end or limit; as, to define the extent of a kingdom or country.*
> 2. *To determine with precision; to ascertain; as, to define the limits of a kingdom.*
> 3. *To mark the limit; to circumscribe; to bound.*
> 4. *To determine or ascertain the extent of the meaning of a word; to ascertain the signification of a term; to explain what a word is understood to express; as, to define the words, virtue, courage, belief, or charity.*
> 5. *To describe; to ascertain or explain the distinctive properties or circumstances of a thing; as, to define a line or an angle.*

But while defining one word necessarily limits it, defining seventy thousand expands the possibilities of language. And his countrymen knew it; the dictionary would become the second most popular book ever printed in English. Despite this success, Webster remained a cranky old man, ranting about Andrew Jackson and the political foibles of his fellow citizens. Luckily, they did not feel the same way about him. He was invited to Washington, dined with his antagonist President Jackson and gave a speech on the floor of the House of Representatives arguing for a copyright bill for the standardization of American English. He avoided his usual diatribes, and the House passed the bill. A month later, the Senate did the same.

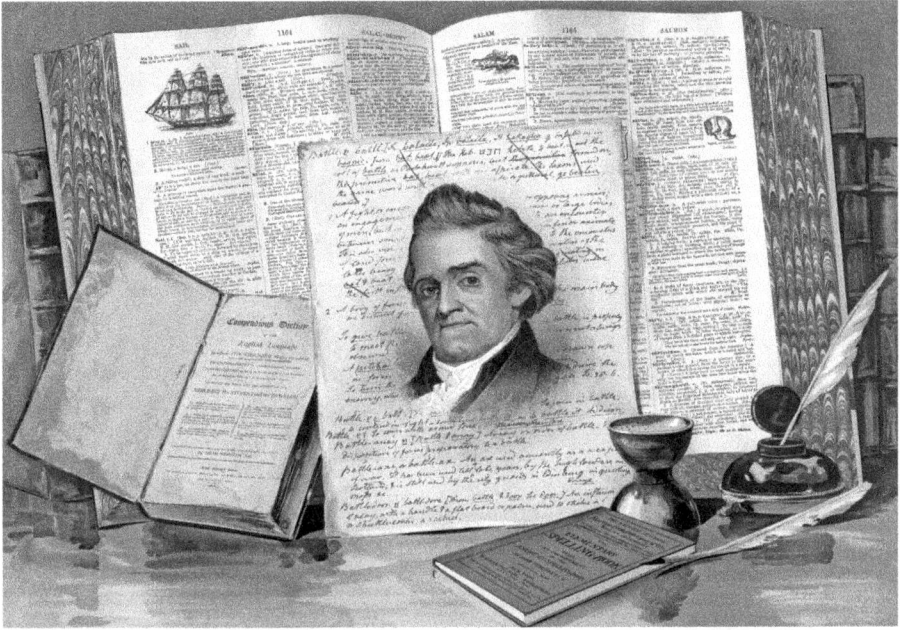

Noah Webster's *American Dictionary of the English Language* established a truly American vernacular, with spelling and pronunciation that distinguished our language from the British. *Library of Congress.*

Finally, on May 28, 1843, Webster passed away in his New Haven home. So many of his generation's literary efforts came to naught. But Webster had lived to see his own triumph, the triumph of a nationally unified language. And his work continued after his death. In September 1858, a Mississippi senator named Jefferson Davis said, "Above all other people we are one, and above all books to be united us in the bond of a common language, I place the good old spelling book of Noah Webster. We have the unity of language which no other people possess and owe this unity above all to Noah Webster's Yankee spelling book." A few years later, while Davis and others rebelled against a unified America, southern publishers continued putting out versions of Webster's "Yankee" classic.

Words seem like such small things, but they matter.

Uncle Tom's Fire Still Burns

G reat literature has the power to change the landscape of the collective mind, halt progression in one direction and inspire new pathways—new loves, new ideas, new morality. A story, as simple as those we tell one another on the coldest of nights around the fireplace, can blow out the fire or start a new one.

When Lyman Beecher brought his family to the "bold mountains and irregular hills" of northwest Connecticut in 1810, Litchfield was the fourth-largest town in the state, a center for commerce and activity. Founded in 1721, this hill town thrived as a thruway between Boston and New York, with tradesmen, artisans and smiths helping the village grow. At the Tapping Reeve Law School, innovations in the training of lawmen were becoming the standard. Down the road, Sarah Pierce's 1792 Litchfield Female Academy grew into one of the primary institutes of learning for young women. With two such reputable establishments and a well-developed marketplace, Litchfield prospered into the first decades of the nineteenth century, exactly as the children of Lyman Beecher were coming of age.

Georgian-style houses and decorative stone walls lined the main roads into and out of town. One of the most prominent residences was that of Benjamin Tallmadge, George Washington's spymaster. A short walk away stood the parsonage house for the Congregationalist minister, a job that Lyman Beecher had accepted. He arrived from East Hampton, Long Island, with his wife and their five young children, settling in the L-shaped house that opened to a grand staircase leading to the second floor. The house would soon need to be updated to accommodate the growing Beecher family, including the future author of one of America's most important novels.

Lyman was born in New Haven on October 12, 1775, just nine months before the Declaration of Independence was penned. When his mother died, he was sent to live with his uncle, who, like Lyman's father, was in the blacksmithing trade. The boy found trade work less than suitable and soon found that intellectual pursuits were more to his liking. He entered Yale at age eighteen, studied with Hartford Wit Timothy Dwight and, upon graduation, went on to the Divinity School. At his first preaching job in East Hampton, he met and married Roxanna Foote, whose grandfather had served with General Washington.

The Beecher family's commitment to religious principles and social justice was legendary. Pictured here with the patriarch, Harriet and Henry Ward were just two of the eleven gifted children of Lyman Beecher, the "father of more brains than any other man in America." *Library of Congress.*

Lyman was a Calvinist, and in his early career, he preached, wrote and published sermons critical of human vices. Among Lyman's orations was "Remedy for a Dueling," written in the aftermath of the Burr-Hamilton clash of 1806. He often preached against intemperance and more often against slavery. He would rear his eleven children with a dedication to God's work, instilling in each of them the idea of hard work and good character as the keys to salvation and building a more perfect world.

Born on June 14, 1811, Harriet was the sixth of the Beecher children and the first to be born in Litchfield. She followed eldest sister, Catharine, born in 1800; William Henry; Edward; Mary; and George. Henry Ward and Charles would also join the Beecher clan before Roxanna died. Lyman remarried Harriet Porter, and soon Isabella, Thomas and James were born. The Litchfield homestead was abuzz with children and activity as relatives and boarders, including students from the nearby academy, filled the house.

For young Harriet, these early years instilled in her a strong sense of kinship and a commitment to others. She also absorbed a love of learning and a fascination with writing from her family. Recalling her father's library, she said:

> *Here I loved to retreat and niche myself down in a quiet corner with my favorite books around me. I had a kind of sheltered feeling as I thus sat and watched my father writing, turning to his books, and speaking from time to time to himself in a loud, earnest whisper. I vaguely felt that he was about some holy and mysterious work quite beyond my little comprehension, and I was careful never to disturb him by question or remark.*

Roxanna died when Harriet was just a girl, and the loss stung. Harriet recalled only a few incidents about her mother that "twinkle like rays through the darkness" and shaped her memory, which she said "had more influence in moulding her family, in deterring from evil and exciting to good, than the living presence of many mothers." Later, Harriet's son would say that she drew on her own mother's death in describing Augustine St. Clare's vivid recollection of his mother in *Uncle Tom's Cabin*.

Harriet began writing both at the Litchfield homestead and when she visited her grandmother's farm, Nut Plains, near Guilford. Even at age twelve, she was writing award-winning pieces centering on questions of fate and the soul, such as "Can the Immortality of the Soul Be Proved by the Light of Nature?" When she heard a reading of the Declaration of Independence, she was moved and stirred toward her life's work. "I was as ready as any of them to pledge my life, fortune, and sacred honor for such a cause. The heroic element was strong in me…and just now it made me long to do something, I knew not what: to fight for my country, or to make some declaration on my own account."

Harriet's older sister Catharine strongly influenced her during childhood. As Harriet's son would say years later, Catharine was a "remarkable woman, whose strong, vigorous mind and tremendous personality indelibly stamped themselves on the sensitive, yielding, dreamy, and poetic nature of the younger sister." But instead of finding herself in the shadow of Catharine's "bright and versatile mind and ready wit," Harriet learned from her and modeled herself after her big sister.

Catharine, as the eldest Beecher child, was constantly exposed to "grown-up" discussions, and her parents did not shield her from any of it. She grew into a freethinker, forthright in her desire "to find happiness in living to do good." Putting her attention toward these aims, she found teaching the greatest reward. Having attended the Female Academy in Litchfield, Catharine moved to Hartford in 1823 and, at a school over a harness store on Main Street, got to work shaping the minds of her students, including her siblings. She drew on the curricula of the Litchfield Female Academy and other schools around the Northeast, insisting that the twelve-year-old girls who entered the Hartford school were old enough to be ready for the rigors of study. She worked multiple administrative and professorial roles, employing Harriet later as a teacher. The school became one of the first in the country where a young woman could receive an equal education.

At age twenty-two, Catharine went to Boston to learn music and drawing and then returned to her home state, where she secured a job at a girls' school in New London. She met and then married Yale professor Alexander Metcalf Fisher, "one of the most distinguished young men in New England." Unfortunately, he left for England and died in a shipwreck off the coast of Ireland. The death had a great impact on Catharine and on younger Harriet. In fact, Harriet would shape her novel *The Minister's Wooing* from the experience of her brother-in-law's shipwreck. She also inherited his collection of books, which included classics like the works of Walter Scott.

Catharine, meanwhile, pondered the very questions about which her father preached. She held her own intellectually and did not bat an eye at those who thought a young woman should do otherwise. Her writing "Biblical Repository" was said to be "the ablest refutation of [Jonathan] Edwards on '[Freedom of] The Will' which has appeared." A local professor told this to a distinguished German theologian, who replied, "You have a

As a young mother, Harriet felt the sorrow of families being torn apart by slavery. She wrote the novel while her own children played around her. *From* Life of Harriet Beecher Stowe.

woman that can write an able refutation of Edwards on 'The Will'? God forgive Christopher Columbus for discovering America!'"

Harriet also absorbed her father's teachings. She pinpointed her own religious awakening to a "dewy, fresh summer morning" in Litchfield, a Sunday when she felt left out of the sacramental ceremony with the "grown up Christians." On this particular morning, when her father began to preach, she was "drawn to listen by a certain pathetic earnestness in his voice." His sermon came from Gospel of John and focused on Jesus's offering of friendship and salvation to every soul. That day, she went into her father's study and declared, "I have given myself to Jesus, and He has taken me." She was fourteen.

What she gained from Christianity was the wholehearted belief and confidence in love: "There is a heaven,—a heaven,—a world of love, and love after all is the life-blood, the existence, the all in all of mind." Her son Charles Edward explains, "This is the key to her whole life. She was impelled by love, and did what she did, and wrote what she did, under the impulse of love. Never could *Uncle Tom's Cabin* or *The Minister's Wooing* have been written, unless by one to whom love was the 'life-blood of existence.'"

Her father's acceptance of a position as president at Lane Theological Seminary prompted him to make a move in 1832 to the Walnut Hills area of Cincinnati. Most of the family joined him, and Catharine opened a female college where she and Harriet would teach. Though Harriet suffered from ill health during the first months in Ohio, she helped her sister plan the school, which would be called the Western Female Institute. While living there, Harriet had her first experiences with slavery, traveling across the border to Kentucky and witnessing things that would later give *Uncle Tom's Cabin* its authenticity. At that time, the city had become a flashpoint for the abolition movement. After a mob attacked Lane Seminary, Harriet lamented, "Pray what is there in Cincinnati to satisfy one whose mind is awakened on this subject? No one can have the system of slavery brought before him without an irrepressible desire to do something, and what is there to be done?"

Harriet married widower Professor Calvin E. Stowe in 1836. The husband of a close friend, he and Harriet comforted each other in grief, and their companionship soon grew into love. She gave birth to twin girls in 1836, a son in 1838 and another son in 1840. While still in Cincinnati, she took charge of a black servant girl from Kentucky. Though she was free by law, they learned that the young woman's former Kentucky owner was looking for her. Calvin and Henry Ward, under cover of night and armed with guns, drove the girl to safety in a nearby town. The Stowes lived near "a half dozen liberated slaves," including Aunt Frankie and Eliza Buck, her cook, whose stories helped give Harriet a sense of what life was like under slavery.

Harriet returned to Hartford in 1842; from there, she wrote to her husband about her desire to devote herself to writing. He gave complete approval: "My dear, you must be a literary woman. It is so written in the book of fate...Drop the E. [middle initial] out of your name...Write yourself fully and always Harriet Beecher Stowe, which is a name euphonious, flowing, and full of meaning."

In 1843, before another daughter was born, Harriet's brother George died. Health troubles and financial problems followed. Her sixth child, Samuel Charles, succumbed to a cholera epidemic in 1849, just before the family moved to Brunswick, Maine, where Calvin had accepted a position at Bowdoin College. But her faith remained strong: "For all I have had trouble I can think of nothing but the greatness and richness of God's mercy to me in giving me such friends, and in always caring for us in every strait."

In 1850 came the debate in Congress over the Fugitive Slave Law. While visiting her brother Edward in Hartford, Harriet learned that his friend had been killed for publishing antislavery papers. Returning to Brunswick, "her soul was all on fire with indignation" at slavery's power over the "innocent and defenseless." Particularly troublesome to Harriet was the way families were broken up by slavers and the brutal way former slaves were tracked down and returned to bondage. The women in her close circle, including her brother Edward's wife, urged her to write about slavery, telling her: "Now, Hattie, if I could use a pen as you can, I would write something that would make this whole nation feel what an accursed things slavery is." She resolved, "I will write something. I will if I live."

In April 1851, Harriet completed the first chapter of *Uncle Tom's Cabin* and submitted it for publication to the *National Era* in Washington. But the novel was not finished, and she needed material, so she wrote to Frederick Douglass, wondering if he could put her in touch with individuals whose stories would help her "make a picture that shall be graphic and true to nature in its details." Her letter to the abolitionist also expressed her ideas about the moral obligation that she hoped her writing would inspire: "The light will spread in churches, the tone of feeling will rise, Christians North and South will give up all connection with, and take up their testimony against, slavery, and thus the work will be done."

The abolitionist movement in New England had been encouraged by the publication of a number of slave narratives, which lent authenticity and pathos to the antislavery cause. When Frederick Douglass published his autobiography in 1845, he gave voice to those who escaped bondage, humanizing Africans in the same way that Harriet would a few years later. Two similar narratives were written by former slaves from Connecticut.

Born in Dukandarra, in West Africa, sometime around the year 1729, a man named Broteer was captured and taken as a slave to the New World. Eventually taking the name Venture Smith, he recounted his tales to Elisha Niles, and the narrative was published in 1798. He tells of his first bondage in Africa:

> *They then came to us in the reeds, and the very first salute I had from them was a violent blow on the head with the fore part of a gun, and at the same time a grasp round the neck. I then had a rope put about my neck, as had all the women in the thicket with me, and were immediately led to my father, who was likewise pinioned and haltered for leading. In this condition we were all led to the camp.*

Eventually, he was bought "for four gallons of rum, and a piece of calico" purchased with the steward's "own private venture. Thus I came by my name."

Hauled first to Barbados and then to Rhode Island in 1737 at age eight, he was taken with his master to Fisher's Island. He married, attempted escape at least once and was separated from his family and sold to a colonel in Stonington, who fortunately bought Venture's wife and daughter later, reuniting the family. Venture earned money and raised two sons, though he would be sold again. Finally, he was able to buy his freedom in 1765 for seventy-one pounds and two shillings. As a free man, he moved to East Haddam, where he purchased his own land. He worked as a lumberman, fisherman and trader in Haddam Neck, where he lived until his death. In his narrative, he reflected, "My freedom is a privilege which nothing else can equal...I am now possessed of more than one hundred acres of land, and three habitable dwelling houses. It gives me joy to think that I have and that I deserve so good a character, especially for truth and integrity." He died in 1805, a landowner who had successfully secured his own freedom and that of his family.

These firsthand accounts highlighted the injustice of the economic system that put prices on men, women and children. James Mars was born into slavery in 1790 at the time when Connecticut was in the process of abolishing the system. Nonetheless, it is important to remember that all states participated in the slave trade, and all states benefited in some ways from the commerce built on slavery. His memoir, *The Life of James Mars, A Slave Born and Sold in Connecticut*, clearly and honestly reports on the abuses, violence and hypocrisy leveled against Africans in the early days of statehood. In 1775, more than five thousand slaves were held in Connecticut. While gradual emancipation began in 1784, freed slaves would be unable to take their freedom out of state. When a young James heard that his master was moving to Virginia, he and his parents fled to the safety of Norfolk, where they stayed for a few years, escaping recapture. By the new law, James could not attain liberty until he turned twenty-five, so he was given to a family in Canaan, then separated from his brother and family and returned to Norfolk to a new abusive owner, "who was fond of using the lash." Hoping to gain legal freedom, Mars returned to his parents, and eventually, the local court had to intervene.

As a free man, married with children, Mars moved to Hartford to work, eventually becoming a prominent member of the community of free blacks. He became a deacon, returning in 1864 to Norfolk, where he wrote his autobiography, published in 1868 by a press in Hartford. In writing it, he sought to correct the notion that New England states, especially Connecticut, were untainted by slavery, "that the so-called favored state, the land of

Dramatizations of *Uncle Tom's Cabin* played well into the twentieth century, though they did not always follow Stowe's original intention. Different productions and scripts might either challenge or support racial stereotypes. *Library of Congress.*

good morals and steady habits, was ever a slave state, and that slaves were driven through the streets tied or fastened together for market. This seems to surprise some that I meet, but it was true." He died in 1880, after voting twice for Abraham Lincoln.

These stories also show the humanity within those who suffer the most and the fundamental worth that connects us to one another. While brutal and disheartening, Venture Smith's and James Mars's narratives show how storytelling is a means to maintain our human dignity. The story of the growing country is a shared story; the power of words cannot be denied. Words help document, bear witness, prove. While a gravestone marks a life permanently—"Venture Smith, African. Tho the son of a King he was kidnapped and sold as a slave but by his industry he acquired Money to Purchase his Freedom"—stories must be told beyond the grave.

Harriet Beecher Stowe knew this. Writing her novel in front of the fire with children playing around her, she was able to speak "to the understanding and moral sense through the imagination...through a series of pictures." *Uncle Tom's Cabin* ran for almost a year, serialized in the *National Era*. The first press run of the book version was five thousand copies, and Harriet received "one copy U.T.C. cloth $.56," the first copy sold. Within four months, she earned $10,000 in royalties. The impact in North America and Europe was profound, making "a series of abstract propositions" concrete. At one time, a London publisher estimated a circulation of one and a half million copies.

In the novel, she weaves the lives of vastly different characters from varied backgrounds, speech patterns and mannerisms. Because her characters are so real, her readers recognize in them the most basic of human instincts: greed, materialism, spite and a will to terrorize, as well as love, dedication, religious conviction, dependencies on abstract economic systems and alignment with familial bonds and kinships. We ache for slaves Tom and Chloe but also for the slave-owning Shelbys and for St. Clare, who are also trapped by the inertia of the system. We are sickened by Legree's unrelenting harshness. Harriet is keenly aware of the variances among the characters; while each might be emblematic of a "type"—the businessman Haley, angelic Eva, moralistic Miss Ophelia, good-natured St. Clair, proud George, forlorn Emmeline, outspoken Cassy and naïve Topsy—each is portrayed fully and whole. Perhaps only pious Tom is one-dimensional.

Dramatizations of *Uncle Tom's Cabin* for the stage followed, the first being produced in 1852 without Harriet's knowledge. However, the plays were incredibly popular, and Harriet could not help but appreciate the impact, as millions more would be exposed to and moved by the story. Eventually, it was translated into nineteen languages.

The book was not the end point of her crusade. She continued to advocate for slaves and for the end of slavery. Many of her appeals were directed to American women:

> *I do not think there is a mother who clasps her child to her breast who would ever be made to feel it right that that child should be a slave, not a mother among us who would not rather lay that child in its grave…For the sake, then, of our dear children, for the sake of our common country, for the sake of outraged and struggling liberty throughout the world, let every woman of America now do her duty.*

She also did small but concrete things like advocating for the Edmundson family, slaves from Washington, D.C. With the help of her brother Henry Ward and donations she raised, the family was able to buy the freedom of their children. Harriet became devoted to their education and personally ensured that they were schooled.

She toured Europe as a celebrity three times, corresponding for years after with people like Elizabeth Browning, Lady Byron and George Eliot. She began writing her follow-up, *Dred*, in 1856. When her son Edward died in 1857, drowning in the Connecticut River just before college, she turned again to writing for solace and motivation, contributing to the *Atlantic Monthly* the allegorical "The Mourning Veil." In December 1858, the first chapter of *The Minister's Wooing* appeared in the same magazine, and *The Pearl of Orr's Island* appeared first as a serial in the *Independent*. All the while, everyone was waiting for the inevitable, as the rhetoric across the country became more and more heated.

When the Civil War finally began, Harriet's son Frederick was one of the first to sign up, mustering with Company A of the First Massachusetts Volunteers. Three years later, he was wounded in the head at Gettysburg. Other Connecticut sons contributed in the war and on the page. Henry Howard Brownell grew up in East Hartford, attended Trinity College and spent the rest of his life in Connecticut as a historian and poet. His collection, *War Lyrics and Other Poems*, drawing on his battle experiences, was published in 1865 and immensely popular after the war. Fellow poet James Dixon, born in Enfield, published poems in *New England* magazine and wrote for the *Connecticut Courant*. He served as a senator during the war, and Dixon's

Returning to her native state in 1863, Harriet moved to Nook Farm, a vibrant community of writers, activists, politicians and artists, including Mark Twain and William Gillette. *Library of Congress.*

signature is the first in the left-hand column of thirty-seven senators to sign the Thirteenth Amendment, freeing the slaves, approved on April 8, 1862.

With fighting well into its second year, Harriet met Abraham Lincoln on Thanksgiving Day 1862. He reportedly greeted her by saying, "So you're the little woman who wrote the book that started this great war." Probably only legend, these understated words were not too far off the truth.

The family finally returned to Hartford after Calvin's position at Andover ended. They sought out the neighborhood of Nook Farm, a cohesive community just beyond the city limits south of Farmington Avenue, west of Sigourney Street and cradled in the "nook" of the winding Park River. Brothers-in-law John Hooker, husband of Isabella Beecher, and Francis Gillette, husband of John's sister Elizabeth, secured the parcel of 140 acres for their own families. Before Gillette purchased the land, he and his wife had used their home in Farmington as a stop on the Underground Railroad. They soon invited other influential politicians, thinkers, activists and writers, all of whom shared the simple goals of living well and changing the world for the better through friendship, community engagement and literature.

Harriet was drawn to the mighty oak and chestnut trees that reminded her of growing up with her grandmother Foote and playing with her girlhood friends. The family purchased the land in 1860, and Harriet employed the builder who helped Isabella and John design their home. In fact, Harriet herself helped supervise the building of the house she would call Oakholm, completed in 1863. Ten years later, though, because of the growth and industrialization of the capital city, the Stowes moved nearby to the Gothic Revival Victorian brick house on Forrest Street across the lawn from the house soon to be occupied by her most famous neighbor, Samuel Clemens.

Following the war, they bought a winter house in Florida to escape the Hartford winters and where Frederick could continue to convalesce after his war injury. Besides the amenable weather, Florida offered another chance for the Stowes to change minds and lives. She joined brother Charles at a school he started to teach emancipated slaves. Ironically, they raised cotton. The shelf of books grew, too. *Oldtown Folks* was published in 1869, the same year she collaborated with sister Catharine on *The American Woman's Home*, followed by *Lady Byron Vindicated* and *Pogunuc People*. Harriet would author thirty published books, numerous short stories, letters, travel reports, hymns and articles for various magazines and journals. She died in 1896 at Nook Farm in Hartford, surviving Calvin by ten years; only three of her seven children outlived her.

Stories matter. Slave narratives like Venture Smith's helped sway public opinion and helped thousands of others tell their own stories of struggle and ultimate freedom. *Courtesy of the authors.*

Stowe burned into us something we secretly know somewhere deep, deep inside: that humans are not always good to one another. *Uncle Tom's Cabin* triumphs, as all great literature does, in its ability to transcend even these vices. We find in Tom's heartbreak our own. We fail him, and yet he does not waver in his faith or in the goodness of handing oneself over completely to that unknowable known. If we are put off by his piety, his absolute, unwavering convictions, it is because we cannot forgive what God can. A trusting Tom acquiesces to his torture and joins Eva in heaven. And there is also redemption. Former slaves Eliza, George and Harry make it to freedom; families—broken and torn apart—are reunited. But Stowe's power, which readers today might find preachy and overstated, is her outright condemnation of humankind. And perhaps she is not wrong. "I wrote what I did," she said, "because as a woman, as a mother, I was oppressed & broken-hearted with the sorrows of injustice I saw."

A *Tramp Abroad* Finds a Home

When Samuel Clemens moved to Connecticut, he had already gotten national attention as a humorist under the pen name Mark Twain. Born into a poor family in 1835 in Florida, Missouri, his family owned slaves, and he spent many boyhood summers playing in the slave quarters, hearing for the first time the "gallows humor" stories he would tell for the rest of his life. After apprenticing to a printer and working on newspapers, he became a riverboat pilot on the Mississippi and joined a Confederate militia during the Civil War. However, he quit after only two weeks and headed west to avoid the conflict tearing apart the nation. He prospected for silver and failed, instead becoming a writer of comic newspaper stories. He had found his calling, and soon he would find the two things missing during his nomadic travels around the United States: a family and a home.

In 1867, he took a steamship tour of Europe and the Holy Land and met a man named Charles Langdon, who showed him a picture of his sister Olivia. Clemens fell in love and, upon his return, began courting the rich girl from Elmira, New York. Meanwhile, he wrote an account of the trip, a hilarious send-up that would become *The Innocents Abroad*. Working with a Hartford publisher, he first became aware of the city, which at the time was one of the most beautiful in America. He had met Harriet Beecher Stowe in 1868, when he was a guest of Henry Ward Beecher in Brooklyn Heights. They had given him a practical instruction on book contract negotiations, something Clemens sorely needed. While in Hartford, Clemens also stayed with Isabella Beecher Hooker and her husband in the Nook Farm neighborhood.

"Puritans are mighty straightlaced and they won't let me smoke in the parlor, but the Almighty don't make any better people," Clemens told his mother. Of course, these "Puritans" he met were the wealthy sort, not to mention artists, thinkers and social reformers.

After lecturing around the country, Clemens had his big break when *The Innocents Abroad* finally appeared in the summer of 1869. Suddenly, Mark Twain became a national name. He and "Livy" were engaged and began to discuss their future. "My future wife wants me to be surrounded by a good moral and religious atmosphere...And so she likes the idea of living in Hartford." Strange as it might seem for this former riverboat captain and western tramp, he had found his home. He was married to Livy in February 1870, and they moved to Connecticut.

In Hartford, Clemens had also met the man who would become his best friend, Joseph Hopkins Twichell. Twichell was born in 1838 and, after being inspired by the preaching of Henry Ward Beecher, served as a chaplain during the Civil War. Now he was the minister of the big Congregational church on Asylum Avenue, and he and Clemens struck up an unusual friendship, hiking up Talcott Mountain to the small wooden Bartlett tower, conversing about everything. Or, if they wanted to mingle with the public, they could walk down Farmington Avenue to a whiskey saloon or to Honiss Oyster House on State Street. They rarely walked to church; Clemens never became a regular churchgoer despite his camaraderie with a preacher. On their walks, Twichell got ideas for sermons and Clemens ideas for humorous stories. Although the minister was a great storyteller, he could not translate his stories to the written page. It was probably just as well for their friendship.

Olivia and Twichell introduced the frontier bumpkin to the genteel social life of Connecticut, something Clemens found enchanting. But to enter this society, they needed to have a place to entertain. While renting a house on Forest Street, Sam and Livy began building an amazing home that would finally be completed in 1874. At 11,500 square feet with twenty-five rooms, it was, by the standards of the time, an enormous mansion. It had gaslights, hot and cold running water, flush toilets, a shower, central heating and a telephone. There was even a burglar alarm but, in an ironic twist worthy of Clemens's stories, no electricians in Hartford to service it. One March night, the alarm went off at two o'clock in the morning, and Clemens joked his wife back to sleep. Luckily, the burglar had "disapproved" of the family's bric-a-brac and never came upstairs.

Along with Colt firearms, a booming insurance industry had made Hartford the richest per capita town in the United States. The population at the time was about forty thousand, and in the winter, as Clemens noted, "most of them ride in sleighs. That is a sign of prosperity, and a knowledge of how to live—isn't it?" The three turrets, five balconies and extensive porch of Clemens's home were another sign of wealth, and Clemens, born in a two-room cabin, was sure to let everybody know. They gave refined dinner parties in the red and gold dining room, and after dinner in the library, Clemens would sometimes dance strange dances or sing popular songs like "Swing Low, Sweet Chariot" and "Go Down Moses." One night, the Clemenses sat with their neighbors Charles and Susan Warner by the bay window of their home and watched a full moon rise. Suddenly, Sam stood up and began to sing "one of them Negro spirituals" in front of the blazing fireplace, swaying slightly, his voice "a whisper of wind in the trees." Then, as he finished, he held his hands to his head, as his housekeeper said, "just as though all the sorrow of them Negroes was upon 'im," singing "Nobody Knows the Trouble I Got" and gave a great shout at the end. It was the serious side of a usually comic entertainer, and no one who witnessed these moments ever forgot them.

Fond of cats, Clemens filled the house with these little mammals. Favorites included a mother cat named Satan and another named Lazy, which he carried around on his shoulder. As children began to fill the house, life became more and more enriched. His daughters Jean, Susy and Clara put on plays

After achieving fame as Mark Twain, Samuel Clemens built his dream home in Hartford, which he called the "chief" example "of all the beautiful towns it has been my fortune to see." *Courtesy of the authors.*

for their father, with his favorite, Susy, striking glamorous Sarah Bernhardt poses. Clemens would make up stories for them about the pictures on the walls of the many rooms. He wrote that the house "had a heart, and a soul, and eyes to see us with; and approvals and solicitudes and deep sympathies; it was of us, and [we] were in its confidence and lived in its grace and in the peace of its benediction."

On the top floor of the house, Clemens built a billiard room that became his study. Far away from the busy first floor and the bedrooms, it quickly became a private domain where fellow writers or editors could visit and where he could swear with impunity. After his family went to bed, he played billiards, sometimes staying up all night and smoking big cigars on the little porch outside his study. And of course, he wrote at a small desk by the porch windows or on the billiard table itself, spreading out his manuscripts and rolling balls with one hand while scribbling with the other.

Clemens believed in Noah Webster's dictum that the American tongue was separate from the British one and argued it clearly and humorously in an essay called "Concerning the American Language." His down-home humor might also have been influenced by fellow Nutmegger P.T. Barnum's autobiography, one of the most popular books of the mid-nineteenth century. Born in Bethel, Phineas Taylor Barnum began to make waves as a newspaper editor and writer and then as an entertainment manager and promoter, featuring various hoaxes and acts before buying Scudder's American Museum. He made his first fortune with Bridgeport's Charles Stratton, better known as General Tom Thumb, and his second with opera singer Jenny Lind. He built what was at the time the most impressive house in America, Iranistan, in the growing city of Bridgeport. He adopted the town as his own, developing East Bridgeport and serving as mayor and as a state representative from Fairfield. He worked to defeat slavery, lectured on temperance and started Bridgeport Hospital. And of course, his retirement project was P.T. Barnum's Grand Traveling Museum, Menagerie, Caravan & Hippodrome, the circus that in various forms would be associated with his name forever.

Despite his astounding career, he also found time to write the startlingly honest *Struggles and Triumphs*. It was a new kind of autobiography, chock-full of funny anecdotes, with descriptions of his flimflams and adventures as an impresario across the world. He described a visit to the battlefield at Waterloo, where the guide boasted to know the location of every aspect of the battle:

I asked him if he could tell me where Captain Tippitiwichet, of the Connecticut Fusileers, was killed. "Oui, Monsieur," he replied, with perfect confidence, for he felt bound to know, or to pretend to know, every particular. He then proceeded to point out exactly the spot where my unfortunate Connecticut friend had breathed his last. After indicating the locations where some twenty more fictitious friends from Coney Island, New Jersey, Cape Cod and Saratoga Springs, had given up the ghost, we handed him his commission and declined to give him further trouble.

The book became one of the most popular books of the century, sold at his museums and circuses, reaching millions of people, including Samuel Clemens, whose wife remembered him reading it in bed and chuckling away. The dry wit and anecdotal structure of *Struggles* would be found throughout Clemens's works, improved on and amplified to its boisterous best by a master of the craft.

After Clemens moved to Hartford, he and Barnum corresponded and visited each other. And Barnum was not the only one. The Stowes lived next door, and the two families visited often. Once Clemens accidentally walked over to see the very proper Harriet Beecher Stowe with "an open collar"; realizing his mistake later, he sent the butler back with a tie in a box, amusing the old lady tremendously. William Dean Howells often came down from Boston, and Clemens returned the favor, one time starting to walk the distance with Reverend Twichell. In Ashford, they met a "seedy old bomber" who ran the inn and talked with "sparkling profanity

Though not remembered today as an author, P.T. Barnum wrote some of the bestselling books of the nineteenth century, including his autobiography, *Struggles and Triumphs*. One of its fans was Samuel Clemens, who would adopt and improve on the style. *Photo by Matthew Brady. Library of Congress.*

and obscenity." Clemens's legs gave out, and they ended up finishing the journey by train. He used the failure as an opportunity to poke fun at himself, of course.

Clemens became involved in the artistic life of the community. With neighbor Charles Dudley Warner, Clemens coauthored *The Gilded Age*, a satirical novel about government corruption and the unfortunate role of big business in politics. And another of Clemens's neighbors was Senator Francis Gillette, whose son William showed promise as a writer and an actor. Clemens loaned him $5,000 to begin his acting career, and at the great author's recommendation, William debuted at Boston's Globe Theater in a stage version of *The Gilded Age*. He would go on to become the most famous actor in the country.

The next two decades in Hartford were Clemens's happiest and most fruitful, beginning with the success of his second book, *Roughing It*. Though many summers were spent at Quarry Farm in his wife's hometown of Elmira, in the summer of 1872, he and his family relaxed at Saybrook Point in Connecticut. But he traveled even farther afield on his lecture tours. Thanks to these tours, Clemens's gray hair, Roman nose, blue eyes and drooping mustache became instantly recognizable to millions of Americans. Unlike most writers, though, he rarely read from his works while on tour. Instead, he stood on the stage and gave what seemed to be impromptu stories from memory, often unpolished and crude, all in a slow, halting drawl, furrowing his brow as if in painful consternation at the strangeness of reality. Audiences ate it up, and he made almost as much money on tour as he did through publishing. Over the next few years, he became both the richest writer in America and one of the country's biggest celebrities.

But his writing had never been more productive, and he continued to pump out book after book: *The Adventures of Tom Sawyer*, *Life on the Mississippi*, *The Prince and the Pauper* and *A Tramp Abroad*. He also wrote the novel for which he would be best remembered, *The Adventures of Huckleberry Finn*. Though Stowe's novel *Uncle Tom's Cabin* primarily attacked slavery, *Huckleberry Finn* attacked the racism that allowed it to exist. The deep ignorance of Huckleberry himself, "educated" by racist adults, continues even after his friendship with Jim, and when he decides to "go to hell" by helping the slave, there is no awareness in the small boy's mind that society itself is wrong. Written in a vernacular English and in unreliable first-person narration, it became one of the rare books to be banned for the various excuses of being smut, of being anti-racist and, later, for supposedly being racist.

Clemens continued to work his satirical humor into serious themes, and his 1889 novel, *A Connecticut Yankee in King Arthur's Court*, originated from his adopted state's new identity as an industrial powerhouse. He probably based the main character, Connecticut engineer Harry Morgan, on real machinist and inventor Elisha Root, who worked for the Collinsville Axe Company and Colt Firearms. Of course, Root was not the only option, since Connecticut was crawling with clever inventors in the late nineteenth century. Clemens finished the novel at his best friend's house on Woodland Street. "I'm here in Twichell's house with the noise of the children and an army of carpenters to help…It's like a boiler factory," Clemens wrote. He said that the carpenters "hammering tickles my feet amazingly" and "jars my table." It was an appropriate atmosphere in which to write the adventures of Harry Morgan and his noisy clashes with the knights.

In this time-travel novel, Morgan is transported to King Arthur's court and quickly sets about improving the Dark Ages for the better. When Morgan sees Camelot for the first time, he asks if it is Bridgeport, a reference to P.T. Barnum's magnificent house, Iranistan. In the narrative that follows, Twain shrewdly lampoons the romances that remained so popular in the nineteenth century with scenes like the "Ogre's Castle," where the Demoiselle Alisande à la Carteloise, nicknamed "Sandy" by Morgan, shows him what she says is an ogre's castle in which princesses are being kept. Morgan laughs, "What a welcome disappointment I experienced! I said: 'Castle? It is nothing but a pigsty; a pigsty with a wattled fence around it.'" When Sandy is unconvinced, he dissembles, telling her that of course he will "rescue" the princesses, who appear to be hogs, from the ogres that appear to be swineherds. He bargains with the men and buys the pigs. And then:

> *I sent the three men away, and then opened the sty gate and beckoned Sandy to come—which she did; and not leisurely, but with the rush of a prairie fire. And when I saw her fling herself upon those hogs, with tears of joy running down her cheeks, and strain them to her heart, and kiss them, and caress them, and call them reverently by grand princely names, I was ashamed of her, ashamed of the human race.*

By the end of the novel, Twain has all but destroyed the romance of Camelot that Alfred Lord Tennyson worked so hard to build up throughout the century. The English were not amused, and Clemens probably lost some of his supporters on the other side of the pond. *The Prince and the Pauper* had already angered a few, and now his satire of the aristocracy and the "glorious past" left them seething. But it was not only the English who came under Twain's satiric pen. Although the "modern" American defeats the knights handily, educates the commoners and sets up a more democratic system of government, his technology causes terrible destruction. In an apocalyptic ending complete with minefields and machine guns, prophesying the horrors of World War I, Morgan becomes little more than a butcher. The gas and smoke created from his own inventions poisons everyone, a grim look into a future that we still struggle with today, prisoners of our own marvelous genius.

Clemens began to pick up a New England accent in the 1870s and '80s and began to have more and more expensive tastes. The parties he threw at his house on the farm became lavish gastronomical events. The lifestyle he and his wife were now accustomed to was draining the bank accounts that had filled up with his book royalties and her inheritance. Worse, Clemens was not immune to the power of illusion, despite having spent his literary life punching holes in other people's fantasies. His foolish investments in a ridiculously complicated linotype machine and a failing publishing company edged him toward bankruptcy throughout the 1880s. Finally, the family had to shut up their beautiful house and escape abroad, a classic nineteenth-century method of fleeing creditors.

Although Clemens had left Connecticut for Europe to save money, he quickly found himself continuing to live the high life. He lectured, trying to make more money, as well as writing *The Tragedy of Pudd'nhead Wilson* and other works. When the family returned to America for brief interludes, they could no longer afford the huge Hartford home and continued to live as nomads, staying with Livy's family in Elmira, New York, or with other friends. Clemens missed his old home and always complained about other places, saying, "How ugly, tasteless, repulsive are all the domestic interiors I have ever seen in Europe compared with the perfect taste of [my former] ground floor." They also stayed in France for several years, renting out the Hartford house in anticipation of someday returning for good. Clemens traveled around the world, sailing all the way to Australia for a lecture tour and writing *Following the Equator*, a more depressing travel book than his previous ones, reflecting his own state of mind at the time.

Then his daughter Susy, at home in Hartford, contracted spinal meningitis. In her fever and delirium, she repeated, "Up go the trolley cars for Mark Twain's daughter. Down go the trolley cars for Mark Twain's daughter." She went blind, fell into a coma and died at age twenty-four, with Joseph Twichell at her side. Clemens was not there himself and reflected, "The burden of

Though the iconic figure of Mark Twain belongs to all of America, Samuel Clemens spent his most productive writing years in Connecticut. *Library of Congress.*

paying, care, misery grows heavier year-by-year." He blamed God, and he blamed himself. And he buried himself in his writing, which became more and more bitter, finding little hope in society or in humanity.

Finally, after almost ten years in exile, in the autumn of 1899, the expatriate returned to America to a celebrity's welcome, with newspapers trumpeting the resolution of his money troubles. But this American hero did not like everything he saw. He became more and more outspoken, disgusted by what he saw as growing American imperialism, by a lack of action toward Belgium's atrocities in the Congo and by the rise in the South of the Ku Klux Klan. In 1901, he wrote "The United States of Lyncherdom" about the activities of the Klan but could not publish it without losing readers in the Jim Crow South.

Another of his troubles was his family's continued rootlessness. They were still nomads, moving between the Adirondacks and Riverdale, New York, while the Hartford house remained unsold. They couldn't go back there, even if they had the money; the death of Susy had ruined it for them. Then his wife's health declined, and they went back to Italy to try to improve it. But she died in 1904 at age fifty-eight. On the night of her death, Clemens went to the piano and began to sing, as he often had in his old Hartford home, "Swing Low, Sweet Chariot" and all the other songs of the happy days. In the other room, his wife told the nurse, "He's singing a goodnight carol for me." And as he did so, she passed away.

Clemens continued to write books like *Letters from the Earth* and a great sprawling autobiography. He traveled with his old friend Joseph Twichell. And in 1906, he moved back to Connecticut, buying land in Redding as a real estate investment and then deciding to build a new house there. By 1908, the large Italianate mansion called Stormfield was complete, and he walked inside and played billiards on his new table. He said, "I realize that I haven't had a real home, until now, since we left Hartford 17 years ago. It is a long, long time to be homeless." He was visited at the new house by such luminaries as Tchaikovsky and Helen Keller. But he would not have long to enjoy his new home. He began to suffer heart disease, the aftereffects of a lifetime of smoking big cigars. His daughter Jean died, leaving only Clara to comfort her father.

At last, on April 10, 1910, his heart began to fail as he lay in his bed at the Redding home. He was trying to read a book, Carlyle's *French Revolution*, and his last words were "Give me my glasses," written on a piece of paper. He took the glasses, tried to read, put the glasses down and, as the sun set outside his window, sank into a final unconsciousness. Joseph Twichell, who had officiated at the funerals of three of Clemens's four children, now had the painful duty of speaking at his friend's, and as the time came to deliver his prayer, the usually talkative man found himself unable to speak. His other good friend, William Dean Howells, wrote a book called *My Mark Twain*, saying, "Clemens was sole, incomparable, the Lincoln of our literature." And like Lincoln, his heirs died out when his sole remaining granddaughter committed suicide in 1964.

The heirs he left instead were literary, including Yale graduate Sinclair Lewis, who continued Twain's battles between the individual and society and continued writing about Connecticut in novels like *Work of Art*. He actually mentioned Twain in eight of his twenty-two novels, and in his Nobel Prize acceptance speech, he said Twain was "perhaps the greatest of our writers." The gallows humor that Mark Twain added to the American literary landscape inspired novelists like Norwich's Wally Lamb and

With sad memories too strong in Hartford, the aging Clemens built Stormfield in Redding, Connecticut, living there from 1908 until his death. *Courtesy of the authors.*

Middletown's Amy Bloom. Newtown's Suzanne Collins would use Twain's mixture of science fiction and social criticism in her *Hunger Games* novels, while Waterbury's Elizabeth Gilbert followed Twain's tongue-in-cheek travel writing in books like *Eat, Pray, Love.* And of course, his heirs spread out to include writers in every country and every language.

In the works of Mark Twain, Noah Webster's dream of an American language came to fruition, and American fiction came of age. In the persona of Mark Twain, Samuel Clemens became America's greatest celebrity author. But though he might belong to the entire country, he lived in Connecticut for the largest and best part of his life. It was the only place that this world-weary tramp really called home, and as he said, "The word never had so much meaning before."

This Is the Women's Century

Female writers were for a long time left out of literary circles or confined to them, as diary writing and dabbling in light verse were acceptable parlor activities. But without more formal networks like those formed by the Hartford Wits, these women had to draw on one another's victories in indirect ways, forging their own paths and picking up trails in other genres besides poetry and story writing. Necessarily, the ones to bridge the nineteenth and twentieth centuries would be writers better known for their political works promoting social change. One such woman was Charlotte Perkins Gilman.

Any undergraduate studying women's literature probably knows Gilman best for her poignantly personal look into the dark world of postpartum depression, "The Yellow Wallpaper." But Gilman's influence on literature and culture is much more widespread. Her inspiration to the women's education, suffrage and labor movements is sweeping yet largely unknown. She would be joined by others who were following in the footsteps of Harriet Beecher Stowe. They were women who put the pen to work for the progress of all women and for the promise of equal opportunities for all people.

Given the lineage into which Charlotte Perkins was born, it is not surprising that she would both aspire to write and significantly push the country, and the world, toward a more humane treatment of all its citizens. Charlotte was born on July 3, 1860, granddaughter of Mary Foote Beecher, fourth child of Lyman Beecher. Mary temporarily joined her sisters as a teacher at the Hartford Female Seminary, which Catharine founded, but had little interest in the work and thereafter stayed mostly out of public life, the least politically and socially active of the Beecher children. But her granddaughter more than made up for Mary's disinterest in the family business.

Like her famous aunts, Charlotte was introduced to literature early on. Reader, writer, editor, critic and librarian, her father, Frederick, helped introduce the decimal system to library cataloguing, and his reference book, *The Best Reading*, became a standard text. Charlotte's mother, Mary Westcott, came from a prominent Rhode Island family, and Charlotte spent much of her youth in Providence, eventually attending the Rhode Island School of Design.

Charlotte's early memories were "thick with railroad journeys" between Hartford and Providence. Frederick abandoned the family when Charlotte was young, leaving her mother grief-stricken and the children without a close paternal influence. Luckily, the family was still close to the Beechers, and Charlotte vividly recalls visiting Harriet's Hartford home with its conservatory, parlor and great dining room. "Aunt Harriet used to sit at a small table in [the] back parlor, looking out on the flowers and ferns and little flowers while she painted in water colors." Young Charlotte—with a kind face; small, studious eyes; slightly dimpled chin; and awkward nose—played with her cousins, Harriet's twin daughters, Hattie and Eliza, and helped out decorating the Hartford house for the election of Grant and Colfax in 1868. For the town parade, eight-year-old Charlotte dressed up as a "Goddess of Liberty" draped in a flag, wearing a white dress and liberty cap and carrying a pole, "which was a new mop-handle with a red-white-and-blue sash tie on it."

As a girl, Charlotte displayed imagination and talent for writing. By age ten or eleven, she had already written her own stories and collected them under the emphatic title "Poetess: Literary and Artistic Vurks of the Princess Charlotte," no doubt affecting an accent she thought appropriate of great artists. At age seventeen, she wrote to her father, outlining her life plan and reporting that she wanted to help humanity. But first she needed to understand history. When she asked him, "Where should I begin?" his recommendations included eight books and issues of *Popular Science Monthly*. On her own, she sought out books on astrology, geology, evolution, anthropology and spirituality, eventually coming to her own conclusions about complex matters: "Soon I realized the importance of religion as a cultural factor but also the painfully conspicuous absurdities and contradictions of the world's repeated attempts in this line." Charlotte's signature ability to evenhandedly analyze the world around her was already apparent.

While her own education was intermittent and self-driven due to her father's absence and her mother's financial struggles, Charlotte's famous aunts and other pioneering women were promoting education, building schools for girls around the state and beyond. At the Hartford Female Seminary, when Catharine found the curriculum dissatisfying for educating the next generation of young girls, she wrote and developed her own. Many Connecticut women made their marks on education and literature, though without famous family names to keep their work in the public mind.

Two poets, Emma Hart Willard and Laura Hawley Thurston, took their Connecticut educations and shared their gifts for education and literature.

Author and activist Charlotte Perkins Gilman was one of the most gifted and influential crusaders for women's rights and economic equality. *Library of Congress.*

Born in 1787 in Berlin, a descendant of Thomas Hooker, Emma worked tirelessly for the "cause of female education" as a teacher. Like the Beecher girls, her path toward education began early, with her parents encouraging her to participate in family discussions and debates. By age sixteen, she was already heading the Berlin Academy, where she began her formal schooling. While instructing there, she also taught during alternate seasons at two other schools in Hartford. By age twenty, she was heading up academies in her native state, as well as in Massachusetts, Vermont and Troy, New York. She believed the education of women had been for too long overshadowed by male-centered philosophies and that it was essential that women learn things like mathematics, which would do more than promote beauty and youth. She penned essays, speeches, poetry and textbooks like *History of the United States, Republic of the Americas.* While her work in education was progressive, her works in poetry were more limited. She wrote one poem commemorating the centennial anniversary of Farmington called "Our Fathers." Another poem, "Rocked in the Cradle of the Deep," captures the rhyme-dominated verse popular in mid-century:

When in the dead of night I lie
And gaze upon the trackless sky,
The star-bespangled heavenly scroll,
The boundless waters as they roll, —
I feel thy wondrous power to save
From the perils of the stormy wave:
Rocked in the cradle of the deep,
I calmly rest and soundly sleep.

Laura Hawley Thurston, born in 1812, grew up in Norfolk in a single-story wood structure down a green lane about a mile from the main road, just outside the village center. Locally educated in her early years, she attended the Hartford Female Seminary and then picked up the torch and taught in New Milford. She gained such a reputation for her methods that she was recommended to head up a girls' school in Indiana. As she shaped young minds, she published poems under the pen name "Viola" in various periodicals. But she never forgot the Litchfield hills. A few stanzas of her poem "The Green Hills of My Father-Land" nostalgically look back on her home:

Land of my birth, mine early home,
Once more thine airs I breathe;
I see thy proud hills tower above,
Thy green vales sleep beneath.
thy groves, thy rocks, thy murmuring rills,
all rise before mine eyes.

While Emma and Laura began their lives in Connecticut, Ella Wheeler Wilcox lived her last years here. Wisconsin born, Ella was a prolific writer as a teenager, publishing poems by the time she finished high school. Her style was similar to Willard's and Thurston's—popular, plain, simply rhymed, typical of the time period and technically uninventive. Her works include *Poems of Passion*, *A Woman of the World*, *Poems of Peace* and *Poems of Experience*. One of her best-known works, "Solitude," however, would give us two very memorable lines:

Laugh, and the world laughs with you;
Weep, and you weep alone.
For the sad old earth must borrow its mirth,
But has trouble enough of its own.

Sing, and the hills will answer;
Sigh, it is lost on the air.

In 1884, she met and married Meriden native Richard Wilcox. They lived in Meriden first and then moved to Short Beach in Branford. There, they built homes overlooking the sound and established Bungalow Court neighborhood, where they hosted writers and artist friends.

Like Emma, Laura, Ella and many young girls, Charlotte wrote poems. When she shared one, her mother contemplated it for a while and then told her to "put on the tea." Though her mom was actually quite supportive of Charlotte and her work, the comment stung, as it would to any budding writer. Charlotte remembered it as an incident because it also spoke of the divide in women's lives—between the tearoom and the writing room—both dually public and private, one accepted and proper, the other accessible only with risk and sacrifice.

The decades before the turn of the century saw a slow but radical change beginning to take shape in women's minds. Gilman observed, "The 'charmer' before marriage and the cook afterward were the prevailing ideas at the time." But times were changing. More and more, women were seen in public occupations, wearing less modest clothing, thinking "radical" ideas. Daring girls talked openly about kissing and participated in "straw-rides" where a "good deal of hugging" went on. Charlotte wrote her first poem, "One Girl of Many," as a defense of the "fallen woman." Physical education and activity began to be stressed for girls: gymnastics, athletics and acrobatics. Charlotte walked two miles to school, did calisthenics every morning and "never wore corsets," developing her own "species of brassiere" with elastic. "Real beauty I cared for intensely, fashion I despised," she said. Keeping up appearance no longer had the sole purpose of winning a husband. A true radical, Charlotte dressed comfortably and felt confident going out alone at night, saying, "If the streets were not safe for women, they should be made so. In the meantime, if there's real danger, let them carry a pistol."

Charlotte met Charles Walter Stetson in 1882, and they were married in 1884. Set on the prescribed path for a new wife, Charlotte gave birth to a daughter, Katharine, in 1885. Unable to recover from growing depression, she soon found herself in a nearly complete breakdown. She captured her experiences later in the fictional "The Yellow Wallpaper." It may be her best-known literary work, and its success shed light on attitudes toward women and their mental health. The unnamed narrator is told that she is hysterical and is recommended to rest and not do any writing. What she had found therapeutic is now off limits. Confined to the upstairs bedroom, she fixates on the dingy wallpaper, hallucinating a woman trapped inside it, and by the end of the story, the narrator, too, creeps along the wall, captured, seemingly insane.

Gilman wrote the story while she was separated from her husband, having left him to go with her daughter to California. Living on twenty-five dollars a month, she was writing short articles, many of which she sold to progressive magazines for a few dollars, as well as poems and verses for children. In 1890, the *Atlantic Monthly* rejected "The Yellow Wallpaper" because the editor said it made him "miserable." But the story was picked up by the *New England* magazine and published in 1891. Even so, one letter asked if "such literature should be permitted in print." Many, however, thanked Gilman for speaking for women and mothers and for others who suffered from depression and societal repression.

The story is a window into the nature of Gilman the woman and Gilman the writer. It is emblematic of the changes that women sought—to be heard, taken seriously, allowed to work and gain domain over their own lives, especially in the home. These would form the foundation of Charlotte's political credo. She continued to write literary pieces—poems, short stories, novels—but her best work is social and political commentary, works that helped usher in the women's movement, the labor movement and even the civil rights movement. She was realistic about her role, though, saying, "No one who sets out to make the world better should expect people to enjoy it; all history shows what happens to would-be-improvers."

Charlotte held a deep-rooted belief in the need for education for women because women's progress was central to the progress of the whole culture; teaching women meant teaching society. Sounding like Aunt Catharine, she wanted to teach them in domestic realms and challenge them intellectually as well. Tackling gender inequality was a step in changing economic, political and even racial inequalities. Many others in Connecticut recognized that education was a means to achieve equal rights for everyone. Canterbury's Prudence Crandall opened her private school in 1831, soon after admitting Sarah Harris, a local African American girl, setting an important precedent as the first integrated classroom. Within a few years, the Canterbury Female Boarding School taught dozens of free black girls. Crandall endured jail, lawsuits and public backlash and closed the school in 1834.

Charlotte attacked social problems from multiple angles; she wrote both creative pieces and progressive treatises. Her first collection of poems, *In This Our World*, was published in 1893. She soon began her career as a public speaker. Lecturing to progressive organizations, she covered such topics as "How to Get Good and How to Stay So," "Heroes We Need Now," "The Philosophy of Dress," "The New Motherhood" and "The Goodness of Common Men." Gilman often referred to her work as "sermons," and money was made through a collection plate that circulated during the events. She aligned herself with multiple socialist organizations, saying her activism was built on "the concern for [the] position of women, and the need for more scientific care for young children. As to women, the need of economic independence seemed to me of far more importance than the ballot."

Initially, Charlotte left suffrage on the back burner. But others worked more fervently on that aim. One of the Beecher girls would be right in the mix, as Isabella became a committed suffragist. Born in 1822, the first daughter of Lyman Beecher's second wife, Isabella was also educated at the Hartford Female Seminary and spent most of her adult life working in Connecticut and promoting women's issues. She met John Hooker, another descendant of Thomas Hooker. John worked in a Farmington office, where Isabella first read about the legal obstacles women faced under the shadow of their husbands, unable to own property without inheriting it or speaking for themselves legally. With her husband's support and legal expertise, she founded Connecticut Woman Suffrage Association in 1869, the same year Harriet and Catharine published *The American Woman's Home*, which instructed women in "domestic science," how to keep a proper kitchen and "to avoid distortions produced by tight dressing" and the "evils of hot bread." Isabella, meanwhile, organized a convention of the National Woman Suffrage Association in Hartford, with keynote speaker Elizabeth Cady Stanton, and she herself spoke at a number of other gatherings. Isabella worked to pass a married women's property bill, finally helping the state legislature pass it in 1877.

For suffragists, the fight was for equal rights, symbolized by the ballot box. For Gilman, she extended her aims to making changes in all levels of society, beginning at home with child rearing and educating parents as much as children. She believed "the first duty of a mother is to be a mother worth having. The second is to select a father worth having. Upon that follows all that can be given in the way of environment and education." About that time, her own mother died, and she sent daughter Katherine back east to live with her estranged father. Like many modern women, she sensed the challenges of trying to do everything. So she put her efforts into ensuring others would at least have an equal shot at having it all. The *San Francisco Examiner* would later ask, "Should Literary Women Marry?" highlighting

Helen Keller lived and wrote for more than thirty years in the woods and gardens of Easton, Connecticut, when she was not traveling the world advocating for children and the disabled. *Library of Congress.*

the chasm inherent in women's struggle: the divide between domestic life and professional life, implying not only that a woman must choose but also that career and family were mutually exclusive enterprises. Gilman's aim was to elevate women to a status where such a choice would never be questioned and women could contribute to both the economic improvement of themselves and of their country simultaneously.

Another fierce fighter in the promotion of equal rights was Helen Keller. Well known for triumphing over adversity, Helen's life and work was spent helping others, especially the most vulnerable, like those with disabilities. Raised in Alabama and deaf, dumb and blind from an illness before the age of two, Helen's life could have become an unhappy tale of a disabled girl sent to an institution, but she did not let things like the inability to see or hear hold her back. A committed family and strong female influences like that of her teacher Ann Sullivan helped shape her into the woman who, like Gilman, was both a celebrity and an advocate for social change. After her book *The*

Story of My Life was published, her fame grew, as did her accomplishments, including lecturing to help raise awareness and support for children with disabilities. Also like Gilman, she aligned with the Socialist Party, for which she was criticized. She worked with the American Federation for the Blind and helped co-found Helen Keller International, an organization that helped those affected by blindness, disease and malnutrition. She also helped create the American Civil Liberties Union and lectured worldwide. But in 1936, she chose Easton, Connecticut, as her home. She named the black-shingled white "farmhouse" Arcan Ridge in the "sleepy town," where she took daily walks along the thousand-foot handrail into the gardens and woods. She spent the remaining years of her life in Easton and died in 1968, a few weeks shy of her eighty-eighth birthday.

Charlotte's lecture tour would surpass even Helen's. On the move for years throughout America and abroad, Charlotte promoted a social philosophy that took a layered approach to social progress and justice: raise the status of all labor workers, especially women, and with those improvements, more would follow in industry, race relations and child development. Charlotte's book *Women and Economics: The Economic Relations between Men and Women as a Factor in Social Evolution* was published 1898, just before the turn of the century, making her even more sought out for speaking engagements. In England for the International Socialist and Labor Congress in 1898, she didn't sign her membership card, disagreeing with the Marxist theories and those who followed Marxism. She attended as a delegate from the Federation of Trade. When over three thousand people attended the Congress of the International Council of Women, Charlotte was among them.

Still unsatisfied with the rate of progress, Charlotte continued to write, adding a new book every few years: *Concerning Children* in 1900, *The Home: Its Work and Influence* in 1903 and *The Man-Made World of Our Androcentric Culture* in 1911. In her lifetime, she would publish eleven books of nonfiction and hundreds of articles and lectures, as well as poetry collections, novels, works of drama and numerous short stories. At age fifty, Charlotte began the progressive magazine *The Forerunner*. Looking back, she remembered an incident at the gym where a circle of young women asked one another what their ideal age would be. While most answered "eighteen," Charlotte said firmly, "Fifty. When I am fifty, people will respect my opinions if they are ever going to, and I shall not be too old to work." Using *The Forerunner* as an outlet, she published creative work, including short stories, novellas and her series of utopian, futuristic novels, *Moving the Mountain*, *Herland* and *With Her in Ourland*, completing this trilogy in 1916.

SHALL WOMEN VOTE?
No; They Might Disturb the Existing Order of Things

Suffragists like Isabella Beecher Hooker and Charlotte Perkins Gilman answered cynicism like this with arguments full of both passion and reason. *"Shall Women Vote?" cartoon. Library of Congress.*

She remained critical of the country's slow progress, saying, "In politics, there seems no great improvement." She joined with fellow writers, including Upton Sinclair and Jack London, and critics like Clarence Darrow to establish the Intercollegiate Socialist Society, later called the League for Industrial Democracy. She served in the National Women's Party from 1916 to 1920. She wrote, "For some thirty-seven years, with voice and pen, I have endeavored to explain and advocate for [economic] change, and the gain made in that time is probably all that could be expected. In so deep rooted a custom as that of to-every-man-his-own-cook."

Even as women gained politically, social progress lagged and brought with it introspective conflict for the newly emerging modern women. As writer Anne Murrow Lindbergh later expressed, "We are working at an arrangement in form, of the myriad disparate details of housework, family routine, and social life. It is a kind of intricate game of cat's-cradle we manipulate on our fingers, with invisible threads. How can one point to this constant tangle of household chores, errands, and fragments of human relationships, as creation?" Charles Lindbergh's wife was a woman of status and could afford the leisure time to ponder these questions. As a bestselling author, she earned fame and popularity outside that of her pilot husband, but she struggled with the demands of public life, motherhood, marriage and creativity. Writing meditatively in *Gift from the Sea*, she longed for time away from her Darien life, for appreciation, for equality. Like Gilman, Lindbergh recognized that women of the twentieth century would continue to wrestle with "how to feed the soul."

Charlotte reconnected with her family in the East and married her cousin George Houghton Gilman in 1900. She and "Ho" courted secretly and then lived in New York City for the first several years of their marriage. With the passage of the Nineteenth Amendment, ratified in 1920, Charlotte was able to participate in the activity for which she and others had fought so hard. In 1922, she returned to "this old Connecticut settlement, Norwich Town," the site of her husband's childhood home. "It has more of the home feeling than such a nomad has ever hoped for...Such nice people." She described majestic old homes that stood back under their great elms and "a succession of noble pictures between the wooded hills and the Yantic River." She lived there with Houghton for the next thirteen years. Shortly before he died in 1934, she was diagnosed with terminal cancer. On August 17, 1935, she committed suicide, preferring "chloroform to cancer," her last willful act.

The lives and works of Isabella Hooker, Helen Keller and Charlotte Perkins Gilman not only coincide with the changing dates on the calendar but also had a significant effect on how women functioned in society and, more importantly, how women viewed themselves. Women of Gilman's generation viewed themselves in terms of community, social progress and purpose. Ever honest in her assessments and provocative in her call to action, Charlotte declared, "This is the women's century, the first chance for the mother of the world to rise to her full place, her transcendent power to remake humanity, to rebuild the suffering world, and the world waits while she powders her nose."

Birth of American Drama

A t the turn of the twentieth century, Americans were mad for Sherlock Holmes. Or at least William Gillette's version of him, the one with the pipe and deerstalker cap, the one that said, "Elementary, my dear fellow." By the end of the 1890s, Gillette had become the most popular actor in the country, making enough money to build himself an eccentric castle in East Haddam overlooking the Connecticut River. His roles in *Secret Service* and *Sherlock Holmes* were the height of sensational production. Along with writing and acting, Gillette experimented with stage effects, lighting and blocking in ways that people thought revolutionary. He also hated "bombast" and "sentimentality" and championed a "naturalistic" style of acting that would become the norm in the twentieth century. But the real revolution in American drama would come from other Connecticut writers, beginning with Eugene O'Neill and Thornton Wilder.

O'Neill's father, James, had been one of those melodramatic actors of William Gillette's generation and had made most of his money playing the role of the Count of Monte Cristo. When he and his new wife, Ella Quinlan, bought a home in New London, they called it Monte Cristo Cottage in appreciation, staying there during the summers and touring the theaters of America during the season. Little Eugene was born in 1888 in a New York hotel and was almost immediately taken on tour with his father and mother. His childhood was not a happy one; his parents were often at odds, and his older brother did not particularly like him. Worse, soon after Eugene's birth, his mother started taking morphine and would struggle with her addiction

Actor and writer William Gillette's *Sherlock Holmes* was the most popular play at the turn of the twentieth century. *Library of Congress.*

Ghosts of Eugene O'Neill's childhood home of Monte Cristo Cottage inhabit the pages of his greatest work, *Long Day's Journey into Night. Courtesy of the authors.*

for the rest of her life. As a child, Eugene experienced regular cases of colic, developed rickets from malnutrition and nearly died of typhoid fever at age two. To soothe his frequent nightmares, his father gave him whiskey.

In 1900, James bought a larger house several doors away on Pequot Avenue in New London, calling the new one Monte Cristo as well. Entering the house and stepping past the staircase, they walked through the front parlor and the dining room into a lean-to kitchen or the living room, described exactly in many of O'Neill's plays. In the backyard, a few large weeping elms shaded the lawn, almost appearing to grab the house. Eugene's bedroom window looked out onto the foggy harbor and across to the huge obelisk of the Groton Heights Monument. He could hear the sad cries of the lighthouse at the end of the avenue guiding ships in through the fog along the wide Thames estuary.

Every autumn, they would leave the house for one of James's endless tours or Eugene would be sent to Catholic boarding school. But at the tender age of fourteen, he convinced his father that he was no longer suited for Catholic school and was sent to Betts Academy in Stamford. His mother had recently attempted suicide, and he barely saw her over the next few years. By his late teens, he was tall, thin and good looking, with large dark eyes and an expressive grin. Unfortunately, he was also beginning to drink, and drink heavily, often to the point of blackouts.

He briefly attended Princeton but failed out, secretly married a girl he got pregnant and continued to drift through late adolescence. Partly to flee his mistakes, he sailed as a working passenger on a commercial sailing vessel, ending up in Buenos Aires before returning to New London. He began watching European plays like *Hedda Gabler* and *The Playboy of the Western World* and was inspired to write a new type of American drama. However, his life remained unhappy; in January 1912, there was an incident with pills that was probably a suicide attempt.

He returned to New London, working for the local newspaper and falling in love with the daughter of a neighboring grocer. His father's career was winding down, and as an investment, James bought a farm nearby that later Eugene would use as the setting for *A Moon for the Misbegotten*. But that autumn, he had developed a bad cough, which doctors first diagnosed as pleurisy. Anxiety about her son sent Ella into another morphine-addled nightmare. But it was worse than pleurisy. Eugene had tuberculosis, and he was sent to a state facility in Shelton and then to Gaylord Farm in Wallingford, checking in on Christmas Eve.

At the time, tuberculosis was the leading cause of death in the United States, and Gaylord was a top sanatorium. Set on almost three hundred acres of rolling farm and orchards, the grounds had a view to the south of the hills of Sleeping Giant. Eugene had an unusually good time there. Later, he reflected that his stay in Wallingford was a turning point in his life, saying, "If a person is to get to the meaning of life, he must learn to like the facts about himself—ugly as they may seem to his sentimental vanity—before he can lay hold on the truth behind the facts; and that truth is never ugly!" He believed that Gaylord had saved him for his future work as a playwright, calling it "the place I was reborn in." Later, he set his play *The Straw* at a version of Gaylord and dedicated a volume of his plays to one of his nurses.

Just a few miles from where O'Neill recovered at Gaylord, Thornton Wilder's family was about to make their home at the north end of Hamden. The wandering family moved from Wisconsin in 1915 into a rented Cape house in Hamden so that father Amos Sr. could teach down Whitney Avenue at Yale. Travel was nothing new to the Wilders, who had lived in places as varied as Hong Kong and San Francisco, as Amos Sr. worked in the consular service. They probably expected that the move to Connecticut would be just another steppingstone, but it turned out to be much more than that.

Encouraged by their exceptional parents to embrace learning and exploration, all the Wilder children excelled in literary pursuits. Eldest brother Amos Niven earned a PhD from Yale, served as an artillery corporal in World War I, wrote poems and essays and ranked high enough as a tennis player to compete at Wimbledon in 1922. Sisters Janet and Charlotte went to Mount Holyoke, while Isabel studied at Yale in the School of Drama. Their mother, Isabella, became the first female elected in Hamden when she joined the school board, a year before women secured the national vote. Thornton's relationship with his mother was tender and lighthearted. In one letter, he extolled her virtues and joked that "if the school knew I spent so much time writing to my mother, I should be fired. From the viewpoint of the schoolmaster a mother is a tiresome nuisance...We only know one kind of mother; others occur in fiction." She was a model and inspiration for him.

Born in 1897, nine years after Eugene O'Neill, Thornton was perhaps the least ambitious of the siblings, though that would change as time went on. He listened to his father's authoritarian advice and studied hard, often teased by classmates for being too brainy. One classmate said of young Thornton, "We left him alone, just left him alone. And he would retire at the library, his hideaway, learning to distance himself from humiliation and indifference." Later, no one would believe how introverted he had been, since he became famous for engaging in conversation everyone he met, from waitresses to kings.

Thornton was at Oberlin College when his family moved to Connecticut but transferred to Yale in part to be closer to them. He met poet Stephen Vincent Benét early in his first semester, and they served together on the board of the literary magazine. During World War I, he served in the Coast Artillery in Newport, Rhode Island, and began writing regularly, publishing his first play. His one-acts were performed by the dramatic association. He even read Eugene O'Neill's early plays, thinking they showed "promise." But he was soon off again, traveling the world, teaching and writing, absorbing experiences that would form the backbone for his life's work.

Meanwhile, O'Neill had left Gaylord a new man, gaining weight and obsessively reading every play he could get his hands on. By the time he returned to New London the following year, he was strong enough to swim naked in Long Island Sound. He stayed that winter in a neighbor's house, where he had the first "ordinary" Christmas of his life, though of course with someone else's family. He would later base his only comedy, *Ah Wilderness!*, on this idyllic experience. He began writing plays, feeling his way toward the dark realism that would become his signature. Leaving Connecticut, he stayed in seedy hotels in New York City, got involved in failed love affairs and lived in almost complete poverty. Finally, he decided he could not go back to New London for summers with his family anymore and left for Cape Cod to join the Provincetown Players. His first true play, *Bound East for Cardiff*, was performed there at the end of a wharf in 1916, and though it did not set the world on fire, O'Neill felt he had found his calling.

Bouncing between Provincetown and New York, O'Neill wrote play after play, many of which were performed at the Playwright's Theater. *Anna Christie* won him his first of four Pulitzer Prizes in 1922. His plays used gritty colloquial dialogue, broken, too-human characters and tense domestic situations to create the drama of everyday life. The 1924 play *Desire Under the Elms* shows a family of puritanical New Englanders in 1850, torn apart by the infidelity of the wife of one of two brothers with the other. Here she confesses to her lover:

> *ABBIE: I—I killed him, Eben.*
> *EBEN: (amazed) Ye killed him?*
> *ABBIE: (dully) Ay-eh.*
> *EBEN: (recovering from his astonishment—savagely) An' serves him right! But we got t' do somethin' quick t' make it look s'if the old skunk'd killed himself when he was drunk. We kin prove by 'em all how drunk he got.*
> *ABBIE: (wildly) No! No! Not him! (Laughing distractedly) But that's what I ought t' done, hain't it? I oughter killed him instead! Why didn't ye tell me?*
> *EBEN: (appalled) Instead? What d'ye mean?*
> *ABBIE: Not him.*
> *EBEN: (his face grown ghastly) Not—not that baby!*
> *ABBIE: (dully) Ay-eh!*

The difference between O'Neill's style and the melodramas of mustache-twirling villains and damsels in distress could hardly be clearer.

O'Neill's plays were already becoming classics, but his personal life continued to cause him suffering. His father died of cancer in 1920 at Monte Cristo Cottage, and two years later, his mother died. His brother Jamie went into a downward spiral of alcoholism and madness and died soon afterward. The entire family had disappeared in three years. By now, he had returned to Connecticut with his new wife, Agnes, buying a farm in Ridgefield, where he hoped he could find peace to write. He was drinking too much again but tried to busy himself with constant writing and psychoanalysis. Finally, in

1926, he got his drinking mostly under control, just as his marriage to Agnes was falling apart. O'Neill sold the farm in Ridgefield and shortly thereafter met a woman who called herself Carlotta Monterrey. They fell in love and took a boat trip around the world together, after considerable scandal and a messy divorce with Agnes.

While O'Neill was defining modern drama, Wilder dove head first into the world of fiction. His youthful 1926 novel, *The Cabala*, saw some acclaim, but a year later he gave the world *The Bridge of San Luis Rey*. Set in Peru in 1714, the novel tells the story of the five people who died when the bridge collapsed and asks the poignant question of whether we live and die by plan or by accident:

> *Some say that we shall never know, and that to the gods we are like the flies that the boys kill on a summer's day, and some say, to the contrary, that the very sparrows do not lose a feather that has not been brushed away by the finger of God.*

The novel was written in a timeless style and showed amazing depth of feeling and thought for someone under thirty years old. It brought Wilder his first Pulitzer Prize and incredible commercial success, becoming the most popular book in public libraries. In fact, it made enough money to allow him to quit his job to write full time. He returned home to Hamden in 1929 and commissioned local architect Alice Washburn to design the house that he would live in until his death. On Deepwood Drive just off Whitney Avenue, the house overlooked East Rock, which Jonathan Edwards had climbed centuries before. Standing above the old Eli Whitney factory, it also had a view of New Haven and Long Island Sound. Wilder's study occupied one of the many rooms on the second floor, allowing a view of the steep private road. There, he would work on his plays, novels and essays for the next fifty years. But he did not live there alone. He invited his aging parents and his sister Isabel to move in with him.

It was very different from O'Neill's experience of life. "My family's quarrels and tragedies were within," he told his son. "To the outer world we maintained an indomitable and united front and lied and lied for each other." And yet, he continued to rack up the Pulitzer Prizes, and in 1936, the Nobel Prize committee invited him to receive the highest honor. However, he refused to travel to Sweden, and when the newsreel cameramen tried to pose a faked scene in which the telegram showed up announcing the prize, he said, "To hell with them!" He and Carlotta reclused themselves from the

The only writer to win Pulitzer Prizes in both the genres of fiction and drama, Thornton Wilder also occasionally acted in his own plays. *Courtesy of the Hamden Historical Society.*

world on a 158-acre estate on the side of a mountain in northern California, as far away from the world of his childhood as he could get. He would not write another play for ten years.

But by now, others were ready to fill his shoes, including Thornton Wilder, who now turned from fiction to drama. He wrote that "the stage has a deceptive advantage over the novel—in that lighted room at the end of the darkened auditorium things seem to be half caught up into generality already. The stage cries aloud its mission to represent the Act in Eternity." It was perhaps a different view of theater than O'Neill's—beyond the pure realism into something else, not the melodrama of the nineteenth century but a new depth of meaning made possible by the examination of "the small details of life" and connection of those details to the eternal.

In 1938, Wilder published *Our Town*, writing in the directorial suggestion that it should be played in a "New England understatement of sentiment, of surprise, of tragedy." Set in the fictional Grover's Corners, New Hampshire, the play mixed the traditional values of small-town America with experimental techniques, including a minimalist set that put the focus on the emotionally rendered plot. The audience is helped along by a "choric stage manager," who states things like:

Now there are some things we all know, but we don't take'm out and look at'm very often. We all know that something is eternal. And it ain't houses and it ain't names, and it ain't earth, and it ain't even the stars…everybody knows in their bones that something is eternal, and that something has to do with human beings.

Wilder had taken the same connections between the mundane and the eternal he captured in his novels and presented them on stage. Audiences responded. *Our Town* became one of the most popular plays in world history, played in dozens of countries on thousands of stages. And it earned him a second Pulitzer, making him the only writer to win for both drama and fiction.

When Wilder's parents died, his sister Isabel remained his devoted caretaker, business coordinator and archivist while pursuing her own career writing novels and as curator of Yale's theater archive. The other siblings also found success. Amos was a Congregationalist minister and professor of theology at Harvard Divinity School. Janet taught at Mount Holyoke and wrote, and Charlotte won prizes for her poetry, unfortunately suffering a nervous breakdown in 1941. Wilder brought her to Deepwood Drive as well.

A day at home went like this: Wilder would drive his Thunderbird into New Haven for breakfast at 7:00 a.m., read the newspaper and stop at the Yale library. He would return to his cluttered study on Deepwood Drive and in one of his faux-leather loose-leaf notebooks copy notes from one into another, revising and improving. After a lunch of sandwich and soup, he might have a beer and take a nap, sleeping for two or three hours. Then it was time for cocktail hour with his sister Isabel and friends or more writing and another nap, before working again in the late night, sometimes until two or three o'clock in the morning.

Meanwhile, behind electric gates at his estate in California, O'Neill fought against Parkinson's disease, his wife's growing addiction to potassium bromide and the intrusion of the world. It was here, in the dark early days of World War II, that with shaking hands he wrote *A Long Day's Journey into Night*. It was, as O'Neill said, "written in tears and blood" and a thinly disguised autobiography—years of pain crumpled into one play. It was set in the living room of Monte Cristo Cottage over the period of a long, drunken day as the family's repressed toxins slowly leak out and poison them. As the mother, Mary, takes morphine upstairs, son Edmund exclaims bitterly:

> *The hardest thing to take is the blank wall she builds around her. Or it's more like a bank of fog in which she hides and loses herself. Deliberately, that's the hell of it! You know something in her does it deliberately—to get beyond our reach, to be rid of us, to forget we're alive! It's as if, in spite of loving us, she hated us!*

We can only hope that writing it leeched the poisons from O'Neill himself. But the last decade of his life was no easier. He and Carlotta fought often in private and public, and in 1950, his older son committed suicide. His own end was not far off, coming at last in 1953. Three years later, Carlotta gave the manuscript of *A Long Day's Journey into Night* to Yale University Press, and it became an instant sensation. Accolades rippled through the world, and O'Neill won his fourth Pulitzer posthumously, securing for himself the throne of American drama. Only Shakespeare has a wider readership among playwrights.

Wilder's follow-up to *Our Town*, *The Skin of Our Teeth*, also broke dramatic ground and secured his third Pulitzer. His circle of friends grew to include people like Ernest Hemingway and Willa Cather, who lunched in Hamden on Sundays. Like fellow celebrities Clark Gable and Don Ameche, Wilder briefly stepped out of the spotlight to serve his country in World War II. He continued to write plays, including *The Merchant of Yonkers*, which won ten Tony Awards on Broadway as *The Matchmaker* and later became the Oscar-

American drama's golden age began with Nobel-winner Eugene O'Neill's gritty, unsympathetically real depictions of everyday conflict. *Photo by Carl van Vechten. Library of Congress.*

nominated film *Hello Dolly!* He also worked on librettos and screenplays, including *Shadow of a Doubt*, filmed by Alfred Hitchcock. An aspiring poet named Edward Albee, who had attended Choate Rosemary Hall in Wallingford and Trinity College in Hartford, met Wilder at a writers' colony in 1950 and showed the older writer his poems. Wilder took him aside, gave him some bourbon and told him that his poems stank. Perhaps he should try playwriting instead? Albee took the advice and became one of the most celebrated dramatists of the twentieth century, yet another to have lived, if briefly, in Connecticut.

Under Wilder's signature tortoise-shell glasses, his eyebrows began to gray toward white. He continued to travel widely: New York, Paris, Washington, Arizona and Peru. But for the aging writer, a place to call home was as important as ever. The comfortable house served as a refuge from fame, where he and Isabel could spend quiet evenings on the patio. He could be found playing music for neighbors or hosting small plays, donating the proceeds for scholarships for local high school students. Isabel would find him musing over the many books in the bookshelf, pensively running his hand over the volumes, "looking—looking for a book that hasn't been written." Sometimes he would drive up Whitney to Mount Carmel whenever the

In his study on Deepwood Drive in Hamden, Thornton Wilder looked into his mind for "a book that hasn't been written." *Courtesy of the Hamden Historical Society.*

words just weren't coming. "When I get stuck, I can usually work it out by walking up to the tower on Sleeping Giant and down again," he said.

Even into his seventies, he continued to write and publish both novels and plays. A brilliant comic novel called *Theophilus North* appeared in 1973, and though he had visions of writing a sequel, it would be his last work. Returning home to Deepwood Drive to a welcoming Isabel one day, he told her, "All the way up the wheels said, I'm going home, I'm going home, I'm going home." He died the next afternoon.

Wilder and O'Neill were both important Connecticut authors with enormous influences on American literature. But their personal lives could not have been more different. Wilder always declared he was "fundamentally a happy person," saying, "Many problems which now seem insoluble will be solved when the world realizes that we are all bound together as the population of the only inhabited star." O'Neill's brutal play *A Long Day's Journey into Night* showed everyone the venomous conflict in the parlor of his family's New London home, the origin of the negativity and gloom that hung over his life.

Perhaps their graves serve as a metaphor for what each man found. O'Neill was buried by his estranged wife in a secret, private ceremony in Forest Hills, Massachusetts, a place to which he had no previous connection. The Wilder family was buried together, under the shadow of Sleeping Giant, near the home they made together.

A Sense of the Now

The great poet Wallace Stevens wrote of his adopted state, "The man who loves New England and particularly the spare region of Connecticut loves it precisely because of the spare colors, the thin lights, the delicacy and slightness of beauty of the place." When he moved to the capital city in 1916, Stevens, like many who journey to the state, came for work. The work he would do here would be twofold: he joined Hartford's growing insurance industry and contributed to the foundations and definition of a new wave of American poetry.

As the nineteenth century galloped into the twentieth, more than just the pages of a datebook changed. With advances and innovations in nearly every aspect of life and ways of thinking, the new century stretched open as a blank, if not scary, slate. Emerging writers would contend with this changing world in changing ways. The era of modernism had begun, supported by poet Ezra Pound's declaration to "Make it new!" Eventually, poetry's shape and sensibility would shift and open. Rhyme and strict meter became less important, though it would be some time before these formal elements became less popular. What also changed was a loosening of inhibitions. As Stevens himself put it, "There is such a complete freedom now-a-days in respect to the technique that I am rather inclined to disregard form so long as I am free and can express myself freely."

But the old ways were not gone, not yet. A poet like Anna Hempstead Branch exemplified the Romantic poetry popular at the close of the 1800s, and her work provides a steppingstone to the poetry that would take shape as the 1900s

THE HEART OF THE ROAD *and Other Poems*

BY ANNA HEMPSTEAD BRANCH

BOSTON AND NEW YORK
HOUGHTON, MIFFLIN AND COMPANY
The Riverside Press, Cambridge
1902

Anna Hempstead Branch's first collection earned her the reputation for being "the Elizabeth Browning of America," but her post-Romantic verse would be left behind once modernism took hold. *From* The Heart of the Road and Other Poems.

progressed. She grew up less than a mile from the banks of the Thames River in the heart of New London. The family home was built by Joshua Hempstead in 1640, one of the only remaining structures to survive the 1781 burning of New London. Born in March 18, 1875, young Anna spent her days among the chestnuts and maples, exploring the world of the family farm, reading and learning. She left New London for Smith College, where she would begin her literary career. Just after graduation, she experienced her first success as a poet, winning a prize for her poem "The Road 'twixt Heaven and Hell," which was published in the December 1898 edition of the *Century* magazine. With awe and terror, a speaker back home in the comfort of bed recounts the ballad of a lone rider galloping into the night. The dark path, "slippery for footing and heavily trod," is full of frightening scenes:

> *Sometimes there was a grinning skull*
> *That I mistook for stone,*
> *And every rock my steed's hoof struck*
> *Was thin like empty bone.*

Finally, the rider clutches a child and is met by a bleeding woman, who eases his wounds with a kiss. With its dark, nightmarish imagery and allegorical tone, the poem expressed religious concerns to which Branch would return often in her work. She would also return to the symbol of the road again and again over the years.

After graduation, she devoted her efforts to the arts, publishing her first full-length collection in 1901, *The Heart of the Road*. It established Branch as "the [Elizabeth Barrett] Browning of America." The title poem from her first published collection explores the road as a means to discovery, the poem written from the point of view of the dusty path. This motif of metaphysical journeying carries through the collection. Her poems often explore religious questions using allegorical narratives to examine spirituality. In one such poem, "Like John upon the Rock," she tells the journey of an evangelist who travels from Idaho to Connecticut to save souls.

She penned a few works for children, including *A Christmas Miracle*, a one-act Christmas play, and *God Bless This House*, published together in 1925; and *Bubble Blower's House* in 1926. She also worked in New York City to establish the Poet's Guild, supporting other artists and poets and serving as vice-president of the Poetry Society of America, the country's oldest poetry organization. But unfortunately for her legacy, she came to prominence just as readers and critics were moving on from narrative and ballad-style verse with traditional structures. Eclipsed by others who came after her, like Robert Frost and Edna St. Vincent Millay, Branch has fallen, to some extent, into obscurity.

Like Branch, Wallace Stevens came of age in the first decades of the new century. Born on October 2, 1879, to a Reading, Pennsylvania family, Stevens grew up in a strictly religious Pennsylvania Dutch environment. His father was a prominent lawyer, stern and opinionated, a contrast to the nurturing sensitivity of his mother. His parents promoted individualism while emphasizing hard work and thrift. With this foundation and against the backdrop of the rising industrialization of the growing nation, Stevens would emerge as a curious, driven and intellectual young man. He was handsome and seemingly self-assured, with his hair parted meticulously in the middle of his head. His studious face showed an intensity that would drive him throughout his life.

Stevens soon left for Harvard, which provided both intellectual stimulation and contrast to his parents' puritanical views. A tension between thought and feeling would pull at the young academic—a tension he would continue to exploit in his poetry, one that paralleled the mindset of the new century. Stevens left Harvard without a degree and returned home to Reading. While home, he met Elsie Moll, and they were married five years later. His father encouraged him to pursue law, rather than literature, and practicality won out over desire. Stevens headed to New York, working briefly as a reporter for the *New York Evening Post*.

That didn't last long, as he felt himself becoming increasingly frustrated with the unimaginative reporting he was asked to do. But he kept up with his father's advice and graduated from New York Law in 1904.

Once married, he and Elsie moved to 441 West Twenty-first Street in Chelsea Square, into a world of work and activity, where he was exposed to the sounds and rhythms of the streets as he roamed around the Lower East Side of Manhattan. In many ways, Stevens was a loner, preferring the solitude of his Sunday walks to company. And the urge to create was strong. "At the library yesterday," he wrote to Elsie, "I felt the need for poetry."

In 1914, he had his first success as a poet, publishing "Phases" in *Poetry* magazine, a publication that issued in the modernist movement, providing an outlet for new avant garde work and showcasing the writers who would be the greats of the early twentieth century. Stevens's poem is imagistic and playfully referential; he manages to splice Paris, London, Agamemnon, hell, Gerard Manley Hopkins and Rip Van Winkle into forty-four lines of lighthearted rhymes:

> *Arabesques of candle beams,*
> *Winding*
> *Through our heavy dreams.*

One might say he was a late bloomer, beginning his career at the age of thirty-five, but maturation, depth of thought and expertise in execution would all be attributes of this "middle aged" poet.

New styles were appearing in journals like *Poetry*, while Branch's more traditional styles in *The Heart of the Road* remained popular with the general public. Likewise, the social and political turmoil caused by World War I manifested as a pull toward the past by some writers, though a counterpoint was provided by poets trying to create a new American voice. Stevens could see the shift and was able to navigate both poles. His poems have a strong sense of music while challenging the reader intellectually. Differences among styles were teased out between Stevens and Robert Frost, as seen in this playful exchange written down by Stevens's biographer Lawrance Thompson:

> *"The trouble with you, Robert, is that you're too academic," Stevens quipped. Frost returned, "The trouble with you, Wallace, is that you're too executive." To which Stevens continued, "The trouble with you, Robert, is that you write about—subjects." Frost finished with, "The trouble with you, Wallace, is that you write about—bric-a-brac."*

Stevens was also divided between two other worlds: the world of literature on the edge of revolution and a domestic world where Elsie waited at home with dinner. He captured this double life in poems that depicted the conjunction of imagination and reality, exemplified by his career as a lawyer and businessman and his imaginative life as a poet. Though one might think that the activity and stimulation of New York City would be a writer's dream, Stevens chose differently—partly out of practicality, partly out of a desire to be free of stimulation—a place where he could be ensured the quiet of a Sunday morning walk.

As his company merged and grew, he transferred to Hartford, splitting his time with New York, sometimes leaving Elsie alone for entire summers. Travel also tore into the time he could dedicate to writing poetry, and often Elsie got the short end of the stick, as he divided his commitments between working on reports to send back to the company and working on drafts of poems. He found his pleasure in imagination, and anything else suffered as a consequence. But in 1919, he transferred permanently to the Hartford Accident and Indemnity Company. The Stevenses were in Hartford to stay, first living at 594 Prospect Avenue and then at 210 Farmington Avenue in a section known as "little Hollywood," a posh neighborhood famous for its upscale residents.

From his house on Westerly Terrace in Hartford, Wallace Stevens trekked nearly two and a half miles every day to work at 690 Asylum Avenue, finding new rhythms and dreaming up metaphors. *Courtesy of the authors.*

Here Stevens wrote the poems that would become his first full-length collection, *Harmonium*, published in 1923. In 1924, he and Elsie moved to their third apartment at 735 Farmington Avenue, where their daughter Holly was born. But it was 118 Westerly Terrace that would be their lasting home. Stevens paid cash for the modest neo-Colonial house and filled it with elegant book and art collections, along with an equally elegant wine cellar. Even so, there was an air of solitude and anonymity within the house. The family rooms remained relatively empty, as everyone escaped to separate spaces after dinner—Wallace to write, and Elsie and Holly to leave him in quiet concentration.

At the office, Stevens was able to wrap his mind around business matters while still creating masterful musings. One of the biggest advantages in this matter was his daily walk to work from Westerly Terrace on the West End to the office on Asylum Hill. This "ritualized" walking became one of his best creative outlets. To his co-workers, he seemed a little eccentric; occasionally, his secretary would transcribe scraps scribbled along the walk. *New Yorker* writer and neighbor Brendan Gill recalled seeing the "forbidding pedestrian," with tailored clothes and neatly parted white hair, make his way, rain or snow, down the street:

> *Rocking slightly from side to side as he lumbered forward, Stevens was as obviously engaged in putting one foot of verse in front of the other as he was in putting one physical in front of the other.* [One time] *he slowed down, came to a stop, rocked in place for a moment or two, took a step backward, hesitated, then strode confidently forward—left, right, left, right—on his way to work. It was obvious…that Stevens had gone back over a phrase, dropped an unsatisfying word, inserted a superior one, and proceeded to the next line of the poem he was making.*

Stevens did not participate actively in a community of artists and writers as his Hartford predecessors Harriet Beecher Stowe and Mark Twain had done. While he did join an East Hartford social group called the Friends and Enemies of Modern Music and the Canoe Club, Stevens preferred to keep a low profile, even as he was gaining a reputation as a poet. While he might not have been a social butterfly around town, he traveled widely for both work and play and maintained correspondence with contemporaries like William Carlos Williams. Despite occasional disagreements, Robert Frost visited, dining with Stevens at Hartford's Blue Plate Tavern, and Carl Sandburg even brought his guitar to play at the house.

Stevens found the city's landscape ample and inviting, particularly enjoying strolls through nearby Elizabeth Park. Translating his reality into poems, he captured the city and the state frequently. In "Thirteen Ways of Looking at a Blackbird," he conjures,

> O thin men of Haddam,
> Why do you imagine golden birds?

In "The Plain Sense of Things," he draws on the greenhouse and pond at Elizabeth Park:

> The great pond,
> The plain sense of it, without reflections, leaves,
> Mud, water like dirty glass, expressing silence.

In "An Ordinary Evening in New Haven":

> The glass of the air becomes an element—
> It was something imagined that has been washed away.

And in "Of Hartford in the Purple Light," he expresses:

> But now as in an amour of women
> Purple sets purple round. Look, Master,
> See the river, the railroad, the cathedral...

Rendering observation into experience is the poet's task. Stevens explained his process:

> A day or two before Thanksgiving we had a light fall of snow in Hartford...I awoke once several hours before daylight and as I lay in bed I heard the steps of a cat running over the snow under my window almost inaudibly. The faintness and strangeness of the sound made on me one of those impressions which one so often seizes as the pretexts for poetry. I suppose that in such a case one is merely expressing one's sensibility and that the reason why this expression takes the form of poetry is that it takes whatever form one is able to give to it.

After the publication of *Harmonium*, Stevens's next collection would be nine years away. In the meantime, other poets were building reputations and

Winner of the Pulitzer Prize for his epic Civil War poem *John Brown's Body*, Stephen Vincent Benét also wrote novels, short stories and screenplays. He is buried in Stonington, where he owned the historic house of Captain Amos Palmer. *Courtesy of the authors.*

gaining readers. Writers like Stephen Vincent Benét wove history into myth, earning critical acclaim and making him one of the most popular writers between the world wars.

Like so many literary greats, Benét's career began at Yale University, and he published two poetry collections as an undergraduate. He served on the editorial board of the *Yale Review* when he interacted with a young Thornton Wilder, working together on the student literary magazine. Wilder described Benét with "hair short and light and curly. His face is round and quizzical and snubbed and his eyes are moles' eyes. He rocks his shoulders from side to side while talking."

Benét enlisted in the army, temporarily interrupting his studies, but still found time to publish his third book before he graduated from Yale in 1919. After working in Washington, D.C., he returned to New Haven for graduate work. In works like *John Brown's Body* and *Western Star*—two book-length epic poems written in what was becoming an antiquated style—Benét created well-crafted, rhyming verse that depicted idealized American characters and themes. Both would win Pulitzer Prizes. Though he spent his short life elsewhere, he purchased the home of Revolutionary-era sea captain Amos Palmer on Main Street in Stonington and is buried in nearby Evergreen Cemetery.

Perhaps not coincidentally, one version of the lyrics to the popular tune that became memorialized as "John Brown's Body" was written by

Connecticut poet and Trinity College graduate Henry Howard Brownell. The tune is an old folk song popularized by the Union army during the Civil War—the tune that Julia Ward Howe later lyricized with "The Battle Hymn of the Republic." While the original Brown was a Scotsman from Massachusetts, the more famous radical abolitionist John Brown was born in Torrington, and for his famous raid on Harpers Ferry, he purchased munitions in Collinsville.

Benét obviously saw merit in the stories that influenced a younger nation and in the need to memorialize without sentimentality. In *John Brown's Body*, he wrote:

> *Sometimes there comes a crack in Time itself.*
> *Sometimes the earth is torn by something blind.*
> *Sometimes an image that has stood so long…*
> *Is moved against an unfathomed force*
> *That suddenly will not have it any more.*

Benét was among the writers who linked old and new styles. However, whereas Stevens's posthumous reputation gained attention, Benét's diminished.

One reason for this was the new writing sensibility of modernism. Lines became less regularly metered; line breaks were less dependent on rhyme. Wallace Stevens, in particular, saw this as liberating, even as the internal structure of his poetry remained complex and intricate. He said these freedoms of technique allowed for freer expression. "The essential thing in form," he wrote, "is to be free in whatever form is used."

Like Benét, Mark Van Doren explored and excelled at multiple genres, making his mark on literature through poetry and prose, creation and criticism. In his poetry, Van Doren worked with traditional forms, like sonnets and quatrains, incorporating modern themes and innovative syntax and line breaks. In "Slowly, Slowly Wisdom Gathers," he wrote, "The web of the world, how thick, how thin, / How firm with all things folded in," comfortable with rhyming line and regular stanzas. As a professor at Columbia University and Pulitzer Prize winner, he influenced many mid-century poets, like future Connecticut laureate John Hollander. His son moved to Cornwall, Connecticut, and Van Doren often visited him there, enjoying the farm and writing during semester breaks from teaching. The landscape of the state influenced many of his poems, and he retired here, dying in Torrington.

In the years between the wars, Stevens continued to establish himself, publishing *Ideas of Order* in 1935. This second collection offered a variety of style and structures as Stevens experimented less with free verse and showed a deft sensitivity to form, including more regular stanzas. His poems continued to hypnotize with deep, imaginative tropes and images. By the mid-1930s, his reputation had been fully established, and the next twenty years would be his most productive.

Still, these were days of increasing tensions. The country would again plunge into war, and at the end of it, the consequences of the nuclear age would shake everyone to the core. As Mark Van Doren wrote:

> *While the world shines*
> *And the rind of it—O, radium*
> *Still does not burn.*

Wallace Stevens wrote to Robert Frost of the turbulent war years, "How nice it would be to sit in the garden and imagine that we are living in a world in which everything was as it ought to be."

The next generation would create modern poetry that "has to think about war / And it has to find what will suffice. It has / To construct a new stage,"

Born in Hamden, poet Donald Hall returned to his boyhood home to read in Thornton Wilder Hall at a celebration of his eighty-third birthday. *Photo by David Leff.*

as Stevens wrote in a poem aptly titled "Of Modern Poetry." In the postwar years, poets like Hyam Plutzik and Donald Hall followed the influences of Stevens. Plutzik was born in Brooklyn in 1911 to Belarusian immigrant parents, and he did not learn English until grammar school, attending a one-room school in Southbury. The family later moved to Bristol, where the teenaged Plutzik had access to books and reading. He eventually earned a scholarship to Trinity College, where he majored in English and began to publish poems in the school's literary journals. He graduated in 1932, heading to Yale for graduate school.

There he would receive the prestigious Yale Poetry Prize. One of the judges was Stephen Vincent Benét, and the two corresponded for many years. Plutzik wrote "Death at the Purple Rim," named after the valley in Connecticut where he lived:

> *This was a little valley all to myself*
> *In Connecticut's northern hills: Cornwall was there;*
> *Warren to westward: Waramaug Lake to the south.*

The poem begins as a tactile reflection on the scenery and then discourses about man's place on earth, invoking antiquity, religion and philosophy. Mark Van Doren described the poem as "strangely and clearly powerful…I have read nothing better in a long while." The poem would win Plutzik his second Yale Poetry Prize.

Like all poets, Plutzik used the one thing that could be relied on in a rapidly changing world: words and their implied permanence. His work captures nature's beauty: fleeting, harsh, recognizable, tactile. Like Stevens, he bridged the old to the new. But readership was changing as poetry became more academic and less popular. Schoolchildren recited Robert Frost, not Stevens's "The Comedian as the Letter C" or Plutzik's "Connecticut Autumn," despite carefully wrought imagery. Nevertheless, the poets of the modern era mitigated a changing world between the wars. Plutzik and others took readers into the Cold War, echoing concern about the changing world. In his poem "Hiroshima," Plutzik asks, "And we behind the man who gave the signal— / How do we sleep?"

While Plutzik was recognized by critics as an important voice during his lifetime, in most circles he is forgotten. Like Stevens, he is a poet's poet. Another author with roots to the state, Donald Hall, has had a broader reach. Born in Hamden in 1928, the year after neighbor Thornton Wilder published *The Bridge of San Luis Rey*, young Donald grew up on the family dairy farm. During the Depression, he attended school as the farm buildings

XI

He rode over Connecticut
In a glass coach.
Once, a fear pierced him,
In that he mistook
The shadow of his equipage
For blackbirds.

The Friends and Enemies of Wallace Stevens commemorate one of his most recognizable poems in thirteen granite monuments along the streets of Hartford that he walked every day to work. *Courtesy of the authors.*

expanded and the cheese, butter, ice cream and, of course, milk became favorites for everyone in town.

With the success of the farm, the family purchased a house in the Spring Glen neighborhood, where Hall attended school and began writing. He often drove into New Haven to watch movies, drawn particularly to early horror films, which in turn led him to writers like Edgar Allan Poe. He confessed that his early poems were "in a desultory fashion because I wasn't sure whether I wanted to be a great actor or a great poet." One of his early experiments in acting was as stage manager in Wilder's *Our Town*.

While still in high school, Hall published with Yale University Press and wrote for the literary magazine of Hamden High School before leaving for private school. Saving up his allowance, Hall purchased the collected poems of T.S. Eliot and, by age fourteen, had decided to delve fully into poetry: "Coming home from high school, I shut the door of my bedroom and sat at my desk, working at poems every afternoon for two hours." The dedication paid off, and the teenaged poet attended the prestigious Bread Loaf Writers' Conference in Vermont, where he met icon and influence Robert Frost, with whom he chatted and played softball.

Hall has an expansive repertoire, with twenty-five collections of poetry and nearly the same number of prose works, including children's and sports books, literary criticisms and essay collections. Most notably, he introduced other readers to American poets through two anthologies: *New Poets of England and America* and *Contemporary American Poetry*. In addition, Hall served on the poetry board of Wesleyan University Press. After nearly six decades with his hands in the evolving world of American poetry, Hall became the fourteenth U.S. poet laureate in 2006.

The poets who came of age after the wars built a network of writers, critics, supporters, friends and, of course, readers. Though their styles differed, they helped one another carve out a nook broad enough to catch some lucky reader. Poets like Benét and Van Doren were showcasing a more traditional verse line and incorporating familiar forms like sonnets and blank verse. Wallace Stevens and others were touting imagism and a break from tradition. Hall helped bridge these gaps, remaining true to form yet opening it. He called himself "a fierce advocate of the contemporary." Hall liked to "play with punctuation, line breaks, internal sounds, interconnections among images." Reflecting on this bridge later in his life, Hall would say:

> *The kind of poem I've taken to writing is something you could call the discursive ode. I call it an ode because although it's lyrical it tries for a certain length and inclusiveness. I call it discursive because it appears to wander, to move from one particular to another by association, though if it succeeds it finds a unity. It tries to connect things difficult to connect, things that at first seem diverse; often the images make a structural glue.*

For a poet, "the greater part of his life [is] conducted on paper." Even into his seventh decade, Wallace Stevens sought out quiet time to write, though he served on prize committees, accepted honors and accumulated awards and put the finishing touches on the *Collected Poems*, which would win him a Pulitzer just after his death in 1955. He wrote, "If people are to become dependent on poetry for any of the fundamental satisfactions, poetry must have an increasingly intellectual scope and power. This is the time for the highest poetry." His adopted home gave him the privacy, images, space and marvelous contrasts that allowed him to shape ideas of order, usher in the modern and help readers make sense of the now. Stevens exemplified the "modern poet," but he also recognized that he was simply a poet of the time, saying, "What he derives from his generation he returns to his generation, as best he can."

Nomads of the Twentieth Century

I n March 1931, modernist poet Hart Crane visited artist Peter Blume at his Sherman, Connecticut home. Crane had been living just across the border in Quaker Hill, but his landlady had ejected him for drinking too much. His friend and editor of the *New Republic* Malcolm Cowley joined them for a party and was surprised to find Crane less destructive than usual, giving away his possessions and seemingly excited about receiving a Guggenheim fellowship. He got drunk during Sunday afternoon, spouting off a "brilliant monologue," and after dinner, Cowley drove with him to New York. As they drove through the dark farmland, Crane wailed, "Oh, the white fences...oh, the interminable white Connecticut fences," as if, Cowley writes, "the fences were an expression of everything that had hindered him from creating a myth for America." Cowley never saw his friend again; Crane left for Mexico to have an affair with Cowley's newly divorced wife and, on his return by boat, committed suicide by jumping into the Gulf. But Cowley moved to Sherman shortly thereafter, saying, "It was a little vision of Arcadia," and spent decades serving on the zoning commission and writing books about the Lost Generation. To one person, heaven, to another, hell; the world, home, Connecticut—all depended largely on perspective.

Many people in the increasingly mobile twentieth century came through the state. In 1939, Truman Capote's family moved to Greenwich, where young Truman worked for the high school newspaper and literary journal, practicing for his future career writing *Breakfast at Tiffany's* and *In Cold Blood*. Some writers were born in Connecticut and moved away, like Stamford's

John Hawkes, while some retired here, like author of *Where the Wild Things Are* Maurice Sendak. Many attended school here, like USA trilogy author John Dos Passos at Choate Rosemary Hall or thriller writer Robert Ludlum at the Rectory School in Pomfret, Cheshire Academy and Wesleyan University, later setting one of his mystery novels at a thinly disguised version of the latter venerable institution. F. Scott Fitzgerald wrote *The Beautiful and the Damned* in Westport. Ernest Hemingway polished up *The Sun Also Rises* in Wilton. And it wasn't only Americans who found a temporary home here. Georges Simenon, the most prolific and popular French author of the twentieth century, lived for a few years on Shadow Rock Farm in Lakeville, using it as a setting for a 1952 novel, *La Mort de Belle.*

The ultimate nomad Jack Kerouac lived in Hartford in the fall of 1941, pumping gas at a station in Manchester. His parents had moved to West Haven earlier that year, and Kerouac had summered there, diving off the seawall at Bradley Point into the sound. Fifteen years later, his friend John Clellon Holmes bought a house in Old Saybrook, and Kerouac returned many times to visit, nearly buying a house of his own in the area. Holmes had been the first author to portray the wandering "beat generation" in his novel *Go*, but for him, and for many others, Connecticut became more than just a place to pass through.

In 1948, a young playwright named Arthur Miller built a small studio on a farm in Roxbury, Connecticut, with the aim of writing the best play he could manage. Two years earlier, he had won a Tony Award for his tragedy *All My Sons*, and expectations were high. In April, he planted a vegetable patch and built a small cabin, raising the rafters and constructing a desk out of an old door. Two lines kept ringing in his head, the opening dialogue from a desperate man named Willy Loman: "It's all right. I came back." He put them in his notebook but did not write the rest of the play until the entire cabin was finished. Then, he began to write, finishing Act 1 in less than a day and the rest in less than six weeks. He called it *Death of a Salesman*, and it was destined to become one of the most important American stories.

Miller was born in Harlem in 1915, the son of immigrant Polish Jews. They built up a respectable clothing business but lost everything in the crash of 1929. Undaunted, the young Miller worked his way through the University of Michigan, finding jobs through the New Deal programs and hope in the promise of socialism. He had signed many protests and petitions and even attended Communist Party meetings. However, at the meetings he attended in the 1940s, instead of the idealism for which he hoped, he found the same programmatic attitudes against which all young men rebel. Furthermore, his artistic passion was viewed by most of the members with suspicion.

He was also finding more happiness in writing. Inspired by Eugene O'Neill's dramatic revolution, he worked with a rough realism to create a tragedy centered on actual life. Miller described the audience reaction: "The audience sat in silence before the unwinding of *All My Sons* and gasped when they should have, and I tasted that power which is reserved, I imagine, for playwrights, which is to know that by one's invention a mass of strangers has been publicly transfixed." Miller had found his calling.

All My Sons had run first in New Haven and earned Miller the attention of well-known director Elia Kazan, who had studied at Yale and founded the influential Group Theater. Kazan's first success had been with Thornton Wilder's play *The Skin of Our Teeth*, and during the summers, his Group Theater troupe met in what is today Trumbull at the Pine Brook Country Club. He brought Miller to Connecticut, something the budding playwright never had previously considered but now saw as a place where he might get some serious work done.

The Roxbury studio "smelled of raw wood and sawdust," while "apple buds were moving on the wild trees, showing their first pale blue petals." Miller wrote all day long, ate dinner and continued to write long into the

Arthur Miller brought all three of his wives to his rural home in Roxbury, Connecticut, including film star Marilyn Monroe. *Photo by Sabrina Walter.*

night, the quiet of the Connecticut countryside helping his process. *Death of a Salesman* owed debts to both Eugene O'Neill's bitter realism and Thornton Wilder's poetic experimentalism. When he finished, he read the play to his wife, Mary, and two friends; they cried, and he mailed it to Kazan. Kazan called on the phone, saying, "My God, it's so sad," and wanted to start casting immediately.

Many people were initially skeptical; after all, the United States was experiencing a postwar boom of consumerism, and few wanted to think about the tragedy of a failed traveling vendor. They were wrong. It became wildly successful on Broadway, winning a Tony Award, a New York Drama Circle Critics' Award and, finally, the Pulitzer Prize—the first play to win all three of these major awards. Miller sent the script to the aging Eugene O'Neill and invited him to see the play, but O'Neill was in the late stages of a Parkinson's-like illness that prevented him from writing or from driving down to see it performed.

In the midst of this, in 1951, Miller met a Hollywood bombshell named Marilyn Monroe, and they had a brief affair. He had made the big time for sure. However, not all the results were positive; the play might have been the first thing that put Miller on the FBI watch list. The feds thought it was a "shrewd blow against values" by a Communist sympathizer. Like many writers of his generation, living through the excesses of the 1920s and the Depression that followed, he leaned left, and in the anti-Soviet feeling of the times, someone like Miller was a ripe target for anti-Communist propaganda.

Then, in 1952, his friend Elia Kazan was called in front of the House Un-American Activities Committee and, in a famous incident, "named names" of fellow Communists in the theater and film world. Miller did not speak to his former friend for ten years, though by this time he had become disillusioned with American Communists and with their hope for the Soviet Union in particular. But he did not like this "naming of names," in which the government forcefully turned people against former friends. The incident inspired what would become his most performed play, *The Crucible*, in which the Salem trials became a symbol for the world of the dangers of government witch hunts.

Meanwhile, Miller had met his most famous neighbor, sculptor Alexander Calder, at a garage in nearby Woodbury. Miller watched as a fire-scarred automobile with wooden-spoked wheels squeaked into view, having no idea that the owner was the inventor of the "mobile." He suggested that Calder soak the wheels for a day and a half, though when he had tried this himself on an old Model T Ford, the results had been less than effective. Despite this bad advice, Calder and Miller became friends, visiting each other's Roxbury houses, the only two non-farmers in town. But not for long. Their confluence brought writers and artists from around the world to this sleepy clapboard community.

In 1954, William Styron impulsively bought a house there with the royalties from his novel *Lie Down in Darkness*. Born in 1925 in Virginia, Styron was influenced by southern writers like William Faulkner. He took an editing job in New York, traveled to Europe, helped found the *Paris Review* and married a gorgeous, wealthy woman named Rose Burgunder. He and Rose found the rustic simplicity of the quiet village of Roxbury a nice change from his former haunts of New York and Paris. Friends like author Peter Matthiessen visited him in his rural getaway, staying up late drinking and listening to Mozart. Another friend, nonfiction master and belligerent loudmouth Norman Mailer, moved to nearby Bridgewater to escape the "beat atmosphere" of New York and visited often—at least, until the two had a fight.

Another of Styron's friends who visited was Robert Penn Warren. Born in Kentucky and usually considered a "southern writer," he actually spent the last three decades of his life in New England, teaching at Yale University, where he had done graduate work back in the 1920s. At Christmas 1953, he moved onto Redding Road in Fairfield, converting a late 1700s barn that housed thirty dairy cows into a home. He and his second wife hosted black tie parties for other authors like Randall Jarrell, John Cheever and, of course, Styron. Warren had already helped found New Criticism and won the Pulitzer Prize for his novel *All the King's Men*, but while living in Fairfield he would win two more Pulitzers for poetry. Then, in 1986, Warren became America's first poet laureate at the same time as he dealt with prostate cancer, a condition that would lead to his death three years later. His last years were spent watching the autumn leaves of Fairfield on brief, slow walks, an oxygen cylinder close by.

Children's author Madeleine L'Engle found a quiet retreat in Goshen in 1952, at a two-hundred-year-old farm named Crosswicks. She and her husband ran the general store, and she served as choir director at the Congregational church. Making her studio in the old garage that housed chickens, she found her peace at "a small brook in a green glade, a circle of quiet from which there is no visible sign of human beings." After literary success, she continued to spend every summer at Crosswicks, and four generations of her family lived under the same roof. The Murry house in her award-winning *A Wrinkle in Time* is based on this Connecticut retreat, and on a dark and stormy night, her young heroes use the fourth-dimensional tesseract to travel from their farmhouse to the farthest reaches of the universe.

Some authors left Connecticut and returned. Born in Bridgeport, Joseph Payne Brennan fought in World War II, earning medals at the Battle of the Bulge. After the war, he got a job at Yale's Sterling Memorial Library and began sending out short stories, poetry and novellas to magazines. In 1952, he sent a horror story to *Weird Tales* and hit his stride. His story "Slime" became an instant classic, its conceit and plot repeatedly stolen by Hollywood and other writers. For forty years, he worked at the library, writing his creepy tales and helping students find books. With over four hundred short stories and thousands of poems, Brennan became one of the most influential horror writers of the twentieth century, inspiring masters like Stephen King. His stories were often set in rural East Hartland or in New Haven, and this made them that much scarier for local readers.

Ann Lane Petry was born in Old Saybrook and attended the College of Pharmacy at the University of Connecticut, working at her family's drugstore. But the "writing life" called her, and she moved to New York. Her novel *The Street* tells the struggles of a young black mother raising a son in Harlem and became the first by an African American to sell over one million copies. Coretta Scott King called it "a powerful uncompromising work of social criticism." Like so many other inherently private people, Petry soon moved back to Saybrook, living in a Colonial house and continuing to write, often portraying her hometown in stories, giving it and the people she knew fictional names. Her novel *The Narrows* was set in the fictional town of Monmouth, Connecticut, and examined a tragic interracial love affair, which in 1953 was a subject of intense controversy. She served on various town committees and remained dedicated to her local community. Her daughter said of her, "My mother wanted to right the injustices that the world visited on people because of their race, or their gender, or their poverty. She became everyone she wrote about."

Many writers found peace and harmony in the natural beauty of Connecticut. In 1959, Pulitzer-winning nature writer and perennial nomad Edwin Way Teale bought a farm in Hampton, deep in Connecticut's "quiet corner," and chronicled it in *A Naturalist Buys an Old Farm*. Teale's dozens of books detailed the natural beauty of America and, of course, Connecticut. He was not alone. Odell Shepard was born in Illinois but after teaching at Trinity College became both lieutenant governor of Connecticut and an award-winning writer, detailing his love of the state's rural beauty in *Harvest of the Quiet Eye*.

Arthur Miller would also discover the natural beauties of his adopted home, but in the meantime, he was concerned with a much more conventional sort. Five years after his first affair with Marilyn Monroe, Arthur Miller left his wife, Mary. On June 25, 1956, he married America's most desirable actress in Westchester, New York, and drove back to Roxbury. As they reached the house, one of the cars of paparazzi following them crashed into a tree, killing the reporter from *Paris Match*. Nevertheless, Miller and Monroe were forced to continue with a press conference in front of four hundred other reporters. Neighbor William Styron witnessed the hullaballoo around Monroe's arrival, noting the "gawking procession of sportshirted Pontiac-ensconced, yowling cretins" that crowded into the town trying to take photos.

Miller's attraction to Monroe might seem obvious, but as she said, "If I were nothing but a dumb blonde, he wouldn't have married me." She read *Salesman* and *The Crucible* and claimed, "I'm in love with the man, not his mind," though she admitted that Miller helped her adjust her life properly. "You're the saddest girl I've ever met," Miller told her, and surprised, she said, "You're the only one who ever said that to me." Perhaps he saw further than the others into her character, or perhaps the others were afraid to tell her. That same year, the House Un-American Activities Committee subpoenaed Miller on a weak excuse, and he appeared, though unlike Kazan he refused to "name names." Monroe joined him at the hearings, risking her own film career and public reputation. The judge fined Miller and blacklisted him, charging him with contempt of Congress. Two years later, his conviction at the HUAC hearings was overturned.

Monroe tried to play hostess to Miller's literary friends, though she wasn't very good at it. However, she did take charge when it came to fixing up another old house up the road in Roxbury. In 1959, she began really going full tilt, contacting Frank Lloyd Wright to design a new pool and possibly a completely new house. The ninety-year-old Wright came to Roxbury and walked around in a western hat and checked overcoat, musing about the possibilities. His plan ended up being far more elaborate than Miller wanted or even could afford. The same year, Miller worked on the script for *The Misfits*, which starred Monroe, Clark Gable and Montgomery Clift. But his marriage to Monroe, shaky already, went into a nosedive, and they were divorced just before the film's premiere.

After Monroe left him, Miller "began to fear I was loving silence too much." She came to visit him one last time, and under the Connecticut dogwoods, they talked uncomfortably. She asked awkward questions about his fruit-spraying equipment. Both silently acknowledged the misunderstandings that had brought them so much pain. Miller said later that she "would exhaust areas of her life. Simply exhaust them. Then she would go on." But she didn't have long to go on. In the early '60s, Miller agreed to work with his former friend Elia Kazan again, despite misgivings about his behavior during the McCarthy hearings. While they prepared Miller's next play, *After the Fall*, news arrived that Marilyn was dead. The play was seen as an attack on her, and it failed.

Miller took an ecological interest in his adopted home, spending his days planting thousands of trees on now barren farmland, reforesting the landscape and pruning the fruit trees in his orchard. In 1962, Miller married photographer Inge Morath in Milford, and she threw herself into life at Roxbury, planting trees with Arthur, taking crisp photos of the many artists, writers and actors visiting or making a home in these hills. He took an interest in his local community, attending town meetings and trying to help the village keep its rural charm. The Roxbury Democrats liked him so much that they nominated him to be a delegate to the 1968 convention, even though he told them to elect his neighbor, a dairy farmer. His feeling about the Vietnam War led him to accept, though without much hope of changing

Secluded and private, William Styron's cabin in the Litchfield Hills brought out his creativity and sheltered friends like writer James Baldwin. *Courtesy of the authors.*

minds. He had already spoken against the war on the New Haven Green and even at West Point. But the convention was a shambles, and Miller "felt totally defeated." It was the last time he became involved in national politics.

Meanwhile, the Litchfield Hills continued to be a destination for authors. James Baldwin wanted to escape New York and came to stay in William Styron's writing cabin in which he wrote *Another Country*. That winter, Baldwin shoveled a path from the writing cabin to the main house and came over for drinks and dinner. Styron's slave-owning grandparents and Baldwin's slave grandparents were an absorbing topic of conversation for the two writers, both trying to find a pathway out of the past. They sat up in the big house until dawn, drinking whiskey, smoking and singing together.

Styron's friendship with Baldwin helped trigger his next novel, the controversial but critically acclaimed *Confessions of Nat Turner*. Baldwin's *Another Country* had brought its own share of controversy, and he came back to live with Styron while the storm about his novel raged. While in Roxbury the second time, Baldwin read the initial drafts of *Nat Turner* and predicted the reaction to it would be even harsher, saying, "Bill's going to catch it from both sides." He was right, and Styron's novel, while financially and critically a success, brought in truckloads of hate mail to the Connecticut countryside. Styron tried to keep calm amidst the political storm he created, taking daily walks in the soft Litchfield Hills. Above the door to his studio, he posted a maxim written by Gustave Flaubert: "Be orderly in your life, and ordinary like a bourgeois, in order to be violent and original in your works." The Roxbury farm allowed Styron to do just that, and his last novel, *Sophie's Choice*, won the National Book Award and was adapted into a film that won an Academy Award for Salisbury, Connecticut actress Meryl Streep.

After being struck down by depression in 1985, Styron was admitted to Yale Hospital and eventually recovered, returning to Roxbury in February 1986, regaining health and balance in his life. He documented his experience with depression in the classic psychological memoir *Darkness Visible*. It triggered a new wave of support for classifying depression as a medical condition.

Neighbors Styron and Miller had long since become friends and over the decades talked often about the differences between dramatic and prose fiction. They were joined by another of Styron's friends, award-winning novelist Philip Roth, who also decided to make his home in the rolling Litchfield Hills. The former Jersey boy found his perfect studio in Cornwall Bridge, a 1790 clapboard farmhouse with a small wooden cabin for writing. Amongst apple trees by the Housatonic River in front of a huge fireplace, on a broad desk Roth wrote dozens of masterpieces. His novels chronicle the immigrant experience, Jewish identity and the changing nature of the American dream. Like Styron's, his novels often pushed boundaries, and his retreat provided safety from the swirling maelstrom of controversy. He continued to produce an astonishing output of books as the years went by, saying, "My goal would be to find a big fat subject that would occupy me to the end of my life, and when I finish it I'll die."

In the mid-1980s, Arthur Miller wrote, "I have lived more than half my life in the Connecticut countryside, all the time expecting to get some play or book finished so I can spend more time in the city, where everything is happening. There is something about this forty-year temporary residence that strikes me funny now." He had almost two decades more to spend here, witnessing changes in the land, like coyotes coming into the state:

> *I am in this room from which I can sometimes look out at dusk and see them warily moving through the barren winter trees, and I am, I suppose, doing what they are doing, making myself possible and those who come after me. At such moments I do not know whose land this is that I own, or whose bed I sleep in. In the darkness out there they see my light and pause, muzzles lifted, wondering who I am and what I am doing here in this cabin under my light. I am a mystery to them until they tire of it and move on, but the truth, the first truth, probably, is that we are all connected, watching one another. Even the trees.*

He continued writing plays, as well as essay collections and an autobiography, and was awarded the National Medal for the Arts and other honors. His daughter with Inge Morath, Rebecca, married actor Daniel Day-Lewis, after meeting him on the film set of *The Crucible*. And Miller's presence in Roxbury brought other actors into the Litchfield Hills, including Dustin Hoffman, whose portrayal of Willy Loman in the film version of *Salesman* had already become iconic. More writers would follow, too, like *Angela's Ashes* memoirist Frank McCourt, making western Connecticut one of the most artistically dense areas of the entire country.

In his last years, Miller battled cancer and pneumonia before finally succumbing to heart failure in the still-quiet village where he had made a "temporary home" sixty-seven years before, the place that had brought him *Death of a Salesman* and the life of a writer, where he had loved and lost and loved again. He had found what so many of these twentieth-century nomads were looking for: a place to call home. And it didn't stop with his death.

Committed to the place he called home for sixty-seven years, Arthur Miller and his wife Inge Morath donated a large swath of forested farmland to the Roxbury Land Trust. *Courtesy of the authors.*

He and his wife donated fifty-five acres to the Roxbury Land Trust, a clear expression of what home means: conservation, preservation, love of place. It was one way to resist the rootless attitudes of the modern world.

Ambassadors of the Muse

O n summer evenings, the Hill-Stead Museum opens its Farmington lawns to the Sunken Garden Poetry Festival. Festivals, really—the series runs every other week from June to August and draws thousands on lawn chairs and blankets, with picnic baskets and sunhats, to hear the country's best poets and musicians. Even the day lilies stay open past sundown. Begun in 1992 to celebrate the spoken and written word, the festival brings recognizable names and budding amateurs to read before the grand white mansion, under tilting afternoon light, deep in the lush foliage of topiaries and blooming dogwoods. The house built at the turn of the last century by Alfred Atmore Pope was designed in part by his daughter Theodate in the Colonial Revival style. Inside, the family's collection of Impressionist and Japanese art fills the rooms, set up as it was when the family lived there. The sunken garden, designed by Beatrix Farrand, is just one acre of the grounds, which offer trails and fields, stone walls, mighty oaks and chestnuts. This amazing venue has witnessed some of our nation's greatest poets.

Connecticut's first poet laureate, James Merrill, read in that green acre of grass in 1993, less than two years before his death. In one poem about his grandmother, Merrill captured the pain of loss against the magical, transformative element of the spoken word, which allows us

> to feel how adult life, with its storms and follies,
> Is letting up, leaving me ten years old,
> Trustful, inventive, once more good as gold.

Even at sixty-seven, his "light baritone, with its urbane accent," captured "an expressive range of inflections," as his friend and fellow Connecticut poet J.D. McClatchy described his reading style. Noted for his sweeping catalogue of work, for both his lyric elegance and intense craftsmanship, Merrill influenced his own generation and those to come.

Born in 1926 to privilege and wealth, Merrill grew up in New York City and Southampton, son of a founding partner in the financial giant Merrill Lynch. Like most budding intellectuals, he was bored by tennis lessons and children's books and yearned for bigger challenges. Even early on, he saw the contrasts and potential of his surroundings:

> *The excitement…I felt in those years came usually through animals or nature, or through the servants in the house…whose lives seemed by contrast to make such perfect sense. The gardeners had their hands in the earth. The cook was dredging things with flour, making pies. My father was merely making money, while my mother wrote names on place-cards, planned menus, and did her needlepoint.*

Even when his mother allowed young James to take a turn with needle and thread, he saw the art, the craft in the process of stitching. "It had nothing really to do with the world, yet somehow…Was it the world becoming art?" Beyond his years, he sought out "grown-up novels" like *Gone with the Wind*, which he read "six or seven times in succession."

Merrill's first book of poems, *Jim's Book*, was written while he was in high school, and he soon left for Amherst, for education, immersion into literary circles and quick recognition. The poems in his first published collection, *Black Swan*, won accolades for the undergraduate, who was "coolly detached and awkwardly self-conscious," according to a friend. He graduated in 1947 after a brief stint in the army during the war and spent a few years traveling before settling down in Connecticut. By that time, he had another collection of poems, one of short stories and a few plays. These would be followed by numerous volumes, reaching multiple genres, but he remained at heart a poet and found himself in the forefront of American poetry for decades.

In 1955, Merrill and his partner, David Jackson, purchased 187 Water Street in Stonington, "the tallest structure in town," four stories high with brown shingles. The property housed the entire block of commercial space and storefronts, but Merrill and Jackson renovated the upper floors with two apartments, using the "exotic duplex" for their living space. The sitting room

At his home in Stonington, James Merrill wanted to "build…a glass room off a wooden Stardeck; put a fireplace in; make friends." He also built a secret passage to his study, hidden behind walls of books, where he crossed out rejected lines with "lithe slashes." *Photo by David Leff. Courtesy of the James Merrill House.*

was full of light and books and fashioned with upholstered chairs, a Victorian sofa, a baby Steinway piano and a "garlic-head" fireplace. Above them was the music room loft with checkerboard tiles and a sundeck, where a "lovely late afternoon, powdery gold above still blue water," allowed for daily views of the harbor. A bust of Roman emperor Otho, which the two found in the basement of Connecticut College, where Jackson taught, stood watch on the deck. Merrill's prized space, though, would be his secret study, hidden by a door of bookshelves, a private place where he wrote poems in longhand, revising carefully with elegant handwriting and symmetrical cross-outs.

Merrill titled his 1962 poetry collection *Water Street* to acknowledge his home. The house was a stop-in for friends like Elizabeth Bishop, who also sought the tranquility of the small town for a few days, or Truman Capote, who summered there. Merrill and Jackson would put on impromptu and amateur concerts and theater productions, calling them "Stonington's One World Festivals," performing works like *The Wasteland* with instruments and song or combining jazz and haiku. To the lively artists, though, Stonington could seem boring, especially in winter, and Merrill and Jackson traveled widely and set up residences in Athens and Key West. Otherwise, the Ouija board came out.

In the middle decades of the twentieth century, poetic sensibilities were in flux. Poets gathered on university steps and crafted edgy poems saturated with the fallout of world wars and the tension of the Cold War, the ironic comfort of the 1950s blowing apart into the turmoil of the '60s and '70s. Such changes opened venues for minority writers and

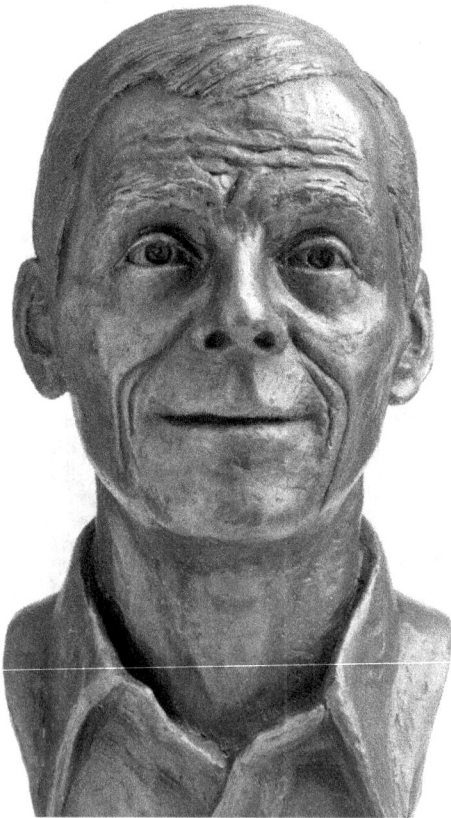

A lover of art, Merrill collected and displayed paintings and sculptures throughout the Water Street apartment, including a bust of himself shaped by artist Sarah Blair. *Courtesy of Sarah Blair.*

women. In the maelstrom of political tension and disorder, Merrill and David Jackson could live openly as gay men, sheltered, perhaps, by a circle of open-minded artists and an art world that was accepting long before the general public would be. Even in the small town of Stonington, Merrill was just the one who drove a Volkswagen Beetle with the license plate "POET."

Connecticut might not have had the recognizable cohesion that formed factions like the Beats, the Black Mountain Poets or the San Francisco School, but it supported a whole network of rising stars, following in the footsteps of Wallace Stevens and marking their own literary pathways in those middle decades of the twentieth century. Merrill explained that he "had been… dazzled by all kinds of things whose existence he'd never suspected," inspired by Stevens and others who experimented with "techniques and forms that could be recovered or reinvented from the past without their having to sound old-fashioned," employing looser rhyme and pointed imagery. He saw Stevens's "great ease in combining abstract words with gaudy visual or sound effects" as an important influence on his own style. And these tendencies would further shape the next generation of poets: "You didn't have to be exclusively decorative or in deadly earnest," he said. "You could be grand and playful. The astringent abstract word was always there to bring your little impressionist picture to its senses."

While the example set by Stevens's innovations with free verse would become the "norm," the richness of form, rhyme, stanza and meter still reigned as foundational elements from which Donald Hall, Merrill and others pooled and wove the next American voice. A long list of poets found their own voices in Connecticut schools and landscapes; many, like Richard Wilbur and John Hollander, would even touch the light at Water Street. These poets felt as comfortable with quatrains and traditional rhyme as they would with sensuous and subtle techniques like alliteration, inventive syntax and diversely broken lines.

Richard Wilbur became the second U.S. poet laureate, following Fairfield's Robert Penn Warren. New York City born, Wilbur attended Amherst, where he met Merrill. From 1957 until 1977, he taught at Wesleyan University and founded the poetry series for Wesleyan University Press. The winner of two Pulitzer Prizes, a National Book Award and many others, Wilbur wintered with Merrill in Key West, often celebrating their March birthdays together.

Woodbury's Hayden Carruth was another Connecticut giant, authoring thirty poetry books, a number of critical essays and a novel. He edited *Poetry* and *Harper's* magazines, as well as the *Hudson Review*. Like his compatriots, Carruth worked with both traditional forms and innovative "jazz like" styles. And like Donald Hall, he was instrumental in introducing new poets to the world through his anthologies, including *The Voice That Is Great within Us: American Poetry of the Twentieth Century*. He often visited his friend James Laughlin's home in Norfolk and titled his 1962 collection *Norfolk Poems*. Laughlin had attended Choate and founded New Directions literary press in 1936, urged by Ezra Pound to do "something useful." His press would publish many rising luminaries from all genres: William Carlos Williams, Henry Miller, Jack Kerouac and, later, Carruth and other Connecticut poets.

Like so many of his fellow poets, William Meredith's connection to Connecticut began when his first collection, *Love Letter from an Impossible Land*, was selected for the Yale Series of Younger Poets in 1944. And like others of his generation, including Wilbur, Meredith's vision of the world was shaped by his experiences serving in World War II. He lived in Uncasville and taught at Connecticut College in New London from 1955 until 1983. Meredith's accolades continued throughout his career—winning the Pulitzer Prize in 1988 and the National Book Award in 1997 for *Effort at Speech*. After a stroke at age sixty-four, Meredith suffered from expressive aphasia, unable to use language to express himself precisely. Such irony was not lost on him—that he would live in a most literal way the poet's dilemma: the "effort at speech."

While critics and scholars found much to admire and praise about the growing showcase of poets around the country, reaching the everyday reader was not as easy. John Hollander, like Hall and Carruth, found success spreading the word about poetry and helping readers understand it. His introduction to poetry, *Rhyme's Reason*, published in 1981, established him as a major influence on readers and poets alike. He wrote:

> *Thinking of my own students, and of how there was no such guide to the varieties of verse in English to which I could send them and that would help teach them to notice things about the examples presented…I got to work and with a speed which now alarms me produced a manuscript for the first edition of the book. I've never had more immediate fun writing a book.*

John Hollander was first singled out for the Yale Series of Younger Poets for his debut collection, and he would later have a long career teaching at Yale and Connecticut College. In 2007, he became Connecticut's fourth poet laureate.

These were among the greatest poets of the century, and they grew together artistically and in reputation. Of William Meredith, Merrill expressed, "I have loved your poems for 40 years." Merrill also dedicated

Since James Merrill's death in 1995, his Water Street apartment has been a place for writers to live and work. You can even try a Ouija board at his dining room table. *Photo by David Leff. Courtesy of the James Merrill House.*

his poem "Dreams about Clothes" to John Hollander and his wife: "Sure enough, a waterfront / Glides into place on small, oiled waves. / Taverns are glittering and the heavens have cleared." They were building their careers, completing manuscripts and teaching students, inviting the invisible muse into Connecticut.

Merrill continued to publish and add to his repertoire. In 1977, he won the Pulitzer Prize for *Divine Comedies*, which included "The Book of Ephraim," later part of his monumental endeavor *The Changing Light at Sandover*. The 580-line epic poem draws on Merrill and Jackson's séance sessions in Stonington using a homemade Ouija board. With a "blue-and-white cup from the Five & Ten" held by Jackson's right hand and Merrill's left, he transcribed "oh, five hundred to six hundred words an hour" of conjured encounters with spirits and muses. Beginning with Ephraim, a Greek Jew from the ninth century, they are joined by spirits of poets, artists and old friends who weave their way through the anthemic, post-apocalyptic chronicle. Merrill's icon and teacher W.H. Auden shows up, as does Wallace Stevens, "with that dislocated / Perspective of the newly dead"; so do Edna St. Vincent Millay, Gertrude Stein, figures from Greek and Egyptian mythology and biblical and ancient ghosts.

Mirabell followed as a separate volume in 1978 and then *Scripts for the Pageant* in 1980, completing the trilogy. *The Changing Light at Sandover* won the National Book Critics Award in 1983. Creatively edited from Ouija transcripts collected over twenty years, the work explores spiritual and artistic questions, eliciting the "powers of lightness, powers of darkness, powers that be." Melodic, narrative and wildly imaginative, the poem has its own internal logic and is built on a belief system that Merrill and Jackson constructed through and onto the board. Tempered with musings on wallpaper and visits from the netherworld, the past is conjured to traverse the present and ease the future.

Though he came from wealth and found success at nearly every turn of his career, Merrill spent only a fraction of his income. He and Jackson traveled widely, yet they lived a modest lifestyle. Merrill firmly believed in lending support to artists of all kinds, creating and funding multiple charities, including the Ingram Merrill Foundation, which provided grants to writers, musicians and artists. He often paid for the printing of his friends' books and was always generous with his time, judging contests, offering feedback on manuscripts and writing blurbs. The Water Street house has been part of a National Historic District since 1978, and since Merrill died, Stonington Village Improvement Association maintains the home, and the foundation offers writers-in-residency programs.

Present and past poet laureates of Connecticut Dick Allen and Marilyn Nelson approach the world in radically different ways. Nelson's poetry delves deep into our shared past, while Allen's exists in a Zen-like present. *Copyright Sarah Bones, West Chester University.*

Promoting artists and fostering their work continues in universities; through multiple journals, magazines and bookstores; and at open mic events and venues like the Sunken Garden Festival. When the state created the position of state poet laureate in 1985, it intended the recipient to serve "as an advocate for poetry and [promote] the appreciation of and participation in poetry and literary arts activities among Connecticut citizens." Merrill and Hollander both served, as have Leo Connellan, Marilyn Nelson and Dick Allen.

Hanover's Leo Connellan was nominated three times for the Pulitzer Prize. He was the poet-in-pesidence for the state university system and served as Connecticut's second poet laureate in 1995, a position he held until his death in 2001. He wrote vividly about the working class, especially about fishermen and workers along the New England coast. As a poet, he tried to speak for those who found themselves marginalized by society, and these instincts led him to promote education. Hayden Carruth said Connellan's "poems [have] a sense of anachronism, a pleasurable nostalgic feeling."

During her tenure as state laureate, Marilyn Nelson worked to inspire readers as an ambassador of the muse. Born in Cleveland, she discovered poetry early, writing, "It was like soul kissing the way the words / filled my mouth" when her teacher picked out a poem just for her, the only black girl in a white classroom. She remained "awed by the power of words." Coming of age in civil rights–era America, moving frequently with her father, a Tuskegee Air Force flyer, Nelson developed a commitment to sharing history that is evident in her eight collections of poetry. As professor emeritus at the University of Connecticut, she is keenly aware of the power of words to teach and inspire, authoring books of children's verse and collections geared toward young readers, like *The Freedom Business*, which translates the story of Connecticut freed slave Venture Smith into verse. She actually made her home in East Haddam, where Venture Smith built his free life. She also founded Soul Mountain Retreat, which offers the solace of the Connecticut countryside to emerging writers.

Nelson collaborated with poet Elizabeth Alexander on *Miss Crandall's School for Young Ladies & Little Misses of Color*, a collection of sonnets that brings the story of Prudence Crandall and the girls of the Canterbury Female Boarding School to life. Alexander creates clear voices that come alive and sing with clarity, images that are vivid and themes that translate across time. She also chronicled the fate of the prisoners of the *Amistad* in a poem sequence published in *American Sublime*. In her eight poetry collections, plays, essays and critical work, Alexander writes eloquently about identity, race, experience and culture. She delivered her poem "Praise Song for the Day" at President Barack Obama's first inauguration, and she is the chair of African American studies at Yale. Of her connection to culture and history, she said, "No matter how devoted we are to the culture and to each other, we have a lot to overcome, imagining ourselves, or imagining each other. And in receiving each other."

Beginning his appointment as poet laureate in 2011, Trumbull's Dick Allen is a poet who shares Merrill's honor for traditional forms while creating his own voice. He was a fellowship recipient from the Ingram Merrill Foundation and taught for thirty years at the University of Bridgeport. Over his long career, Allen has meditatively captured the quiet and the sacred sounds of the world as experienced in the last stanza of "On the New Haven Line":

> *This is the day. You might have died*
> *And never seen Rowayton in the rain*
> *Or morning glories bloom in Darien.*
> *This is the day you might have died.*

His meditations on the human experience lent comfort to the state and beyond with the poem "Solace" in the wake of the Sandy Hook School massacre, with quiet, understated repetition:

No small hand will go unheld
No voice unheard is ever lost
In the snow lightly falling
In the snow lightly falling

His subtlety and attention to cadence reach audiences, and his poems establish that the muse is not far off but within and about us every day and everywhere.

These writers reflect a diverse range of styles, and their work as ambassadors of poetry highlights Connecticut's contributions to an active world of literature. James Merrill's *The Changing Light at Sandover* is an epic endeavor, on par in scope with T.S. Eliot's *The Wasteland* and Ezra Pound's *Cantos*. And shouldn't we want our literary guides to be this ambitious? Unfortunately, few will read the entirety; page through it, yes, but delve head first into it without the promptings of a graduate thesis, probably not. However, the chances that readers will encounter something they can tap

Set on the grounds of the Hill-Stead Museum in Farmington, the Sunken Garden Poetry Festival welcomes the country's best poets and musicians, as well as thousands of listeners. *Photo by David Leff.*

into are good, with the vast network of universities and colleges and an equally vast number of elementary and high school teachers who have not yet given up on the power of poetry. Indeed, as Dick Allen writes, "All the children who were poets" will be able to "lie on their backs; / smiling and singing together, they bring forth the stars."

The Changing Light at Sandover is really about the power of the muse. Every true citizen attempts to tap into the past, and all societies search for suitable chaperones to help navigate it. Merrill prompted, "Don't you think there comes a time when everyone, not just a poet, wants to get beyond the Self? To reach, if you like, the 'god' within you?" And of the muses Merrill sought, he said, "Whenever we needed them, there they were; and a large part of that wonder was to feel how deeply they needed us." They show up in person at readings every weekend around the state and every summer in a sunken garden in Farmington. Bring your blanket; the ambassadors of the muse need you. Ouija unnecessary.

Into the New Millennium

In *The Bridge of San Luis Rey*, Thornton Wilder writes that "the art of biography is more difficult than is generally supposed." And when that biography is of dozens of Connecticut authors, over hundreds of years, it is even more difficult to give everyone their due. But hopefully you have encountered a few neighbors you want to know better.

As you've met each of these authors, you might have seen reflections of your own life. At the next family dinner, you might be reminded of the Beechers and mercifully not the O'Neills. Maybe you'll decide to walk a few city blocks with Wallace Stevens, sit in an old church pew with Jonathan Edwards or play a game of billiards with Samuel Clemens. Maybe you've been moved to stand up at a rally with Charlotte Perkins Gilman or argue at a town council meeting with Arthur Miller.

With any luck, you've been inspired to actually read these writers who share your home. As Clemens's alter ego, Mark Twain, put it, "The man who does not read good books has no advantage over the man who *can't* read them." And reading is not the end of your experience. You can watch a play at one of our dozens of theaters or enjoy a poetry reading at a local library. Let the words of your neighbors seep into your heart and bubble in your mind until they *become your words*.

After all, as Noah Webster said, "Language is not an abstract construction of the learned, or of dictionary makers, but is something arising out of the work, needs, ties, joys, affections, tastes, of long generations of humanity, and has its bases broad and low, close to the ground." When you are full of this new, sweet language, you could even send it on, write it down, add your voice to the great murmuring Connecticut River of voices.

Through words, make the new millennium your own.

Selected Sources

Academy of American Poets. http://www.poets.org.

Alexander, Elizabeth. *Crave Radiance: New and Selected Poems, 1990–2010.* Minneapolis, MN: Graywolf Press, 2010.

Allen, Dick. "Overcoming the Tic of Techniques: The Emergence of Expansive Poetry." Expansive Poetry and Music Online. http://www.expansivepoetryonline.com.

———. "Solace." From "A Simple, Solemn Tribute to Sandy Hook Victims," by Ray Hardman. WNPR.org. http://www.wnpr.org (accessed December 11, 2013).

Barnum, P.T. *Struggles and Triumphs.* Author's edition. Buffalo, NY: Courier Company, 1882.

Barone, Dennis, ed. *Garnet Poems: An Anthology of Connecticut Poetry Since 1776.* Middletown, CT: Wesleyan University Press, 2012.

Beers, Henry. *The Connecticut Wits and Other Essays.* New Haven, CT: Yale University Press, 1920.

Benét, Stephen Vincent. *John Brown's Body.* Chicago: Ivan R. Dee, Inc., 1928.

Berg, Gordon. "'John Brown's Body'—Stephen Vincent Benét and Civil War Memory." Weider History Network. www.historynet.com (accessed February 12, 2012).

Bigsby, Christopher. *Arthur Miller, 1915–1962.* Cambridge, MA: Harvard University Press, 2009.

Black, Stephen. *Eugene O'Neill: Beyond Mourning and Tragedy.* New Haven, CT: Yale University Press, 1999.

Blotner, Joseph. *Robert Penn Warren: A Biography*. New York: Random House, 1997.

Bowden, Edwin, ed. *The Satiric Poems of John Trumbull*. Austin: University of Texas Press, 1963.

Bradley, Sculley. "Review of Last Poems of Anna Hempstead Branch." *American Literature* 17, no. 2 (May 1945): 190–92.

Branch, Anna Hempstead. *The Heart of the Road and Other Poems*. New York: Houghton Mifflin and Co., 1902.

———. "The Road 'Twixt Heaven and Hell." *Century Magazine* 57, no. 39 (December 1898): 305–7.

Bucco, Martin. "Mark Twain and Sinclair Lewis." *American Literary Realism, 1870–1910* 31, no. 3 (Spring 1999).

Carruth, Hayden. "[Leo Connellan's] First Selected Poems." *New York Times Book Review*. May 23, 1976, BR10. http://www.newyorktimes.com.

Courtney, Steve. *Joseph Hopkins Twichell*. Athens: University of Georgia Press, 2008.

Cowley, Malcolm. *A Second Flowering: Works and Days of the Lost Generation*. New York: Viking Press, 1973.

Dailey, Jan. "At Home With Philip Roth." Slate.com (accessed June 26, 2011).

Davis, Brad, ed. *Sunken Garden Poetry, 1992–2012*. Middletown, CT: Wesleyan University Press, 2012.

DeLuca, Richard. "Sarah Kemble Knight's Journey through Connecticut." Connecticut History Online. Connecticut Humanities. http://www.connecticuthistory.org.

De Simone, Deborah M. "Charlotte Perkins Gilman and the Feminization of Education." Women in Literature and Life Assembly of the National Council of Teachers of English. Edited by Patricia Kelly. Fall 2005, 13–17.

Dwight, Timothy. *Travels in New England and New York*. London: William Baynes and Son, 1828.

Edwards, Jonathan. *The Collected Works of Jonathan Edwards*. Edited by Wilson Kimnach and Kenneth Minkema et al. Vols. 1–25. New Haven, CT: Yale University Press, multiple years.

Eldridge, Joseph. *History of Norfolk, Litchfield County, Connecticut*. Everett: Massachusetts Publishing Company, 1900.

Ellsworth, Mary Ellen. "A Connecticut Feminist Prophet." *Connecticut Explored* 10, no. 1 (Winter 2011–12): 25–29.

Everett, Charles W., ed. *The Poets of Connecticut; with Biographical Sketches*. Hartford, CT: Case, Tiffany and Burnham, 1846.

Frank, Jenifer. "Hartford's Nook Farm." Connecticut History Online. Connecticut Humanities. http://www.connecticuthistory.org.

Gelb, Arthur, and Barbara Gelb. *O'Neill: Life with Monte Cristo*. New York: Applause Books, 2000.

Gilbert, Sandra M., and Susan Gubar, eds. *The Norton Anthology of Literature by Women: The Tradition in English*. 1st ed. New York: W.W. Norton, 1985, 1337–8.

Gilman, Charlotte Perkins. *The Living of Charlotte Perkins Gilman: An Autobiography*. Introduction by Anne J. Lane. Madison: University of Wisconsin Press, 1935.

———. "The Yellow Wallpaper." Project Gutenberg. http://gutenberg.org.

Haas, Irvin. *Historic Homes of American Authors*. Washington, D.C.: Preservation Press, 1991, 29.

Haight, Gordon. *Mrs. Sigourney: The Sweet Singer of Hartford*. New Haven, CT: Yale University Press, 1930.

Hall, Donald. Interview with Peter Stitt. "The Art of Poetry, No. 43." *Paris Review* 120 (Fall 1991).

———, ed. *The Oxford Book of American Literary Anecdotes*. New York: Oxford University Press, 1981.

"Harriet Beecher Stowe's Life." Harriet Beecher Stowe Center. http://harrietbeecherstowecenter.org.

Harrison, Gilbert. *The Enthusiast: A Life of Thornton Wilder*. New Haven, CT: Ticknor and Fields, 1983.

Hedrick, Joan D. *Harriet Beecher Stowe: A Life*. New York: Oxford University Press, 1994.

Hinks, Peter P. "James Mars' Words Illuminate the Cruelty of Slavery in New England." Connecticut History Online. Connecticut Humanities. http://www.connectiuthistory.org.

History of Litchfield County, Connecticut, with Illustrations and Biographical Sketches of the Prominent Men and Pioneers. Philadelphia: J.W. Lewis and Co., 1881.

Howard, Leon. *The Connecticut Wits*. Chicago: University of Chicago, 1943.

Hurd, D. Hamilton. *History of New London County*. Philadelphia: J.W. Lewis, 1882.

Kaplan, Fred. *The Singular Mark Twain*. New York: Doubleday, 2003.

Kendall, Joshua. *The Forgotten Founding Father: Noah Webster's Obsession and the Creation of an American Culture*. New York: G.P. Putnam's Sons, 2010.

Knight, Sarah. *The Private Journal of a Journey from Boston to New York, in the Year 1704, Kept by Madam Knight*. Albany, NY: Frank H. Little, 1865.

Krieg, Joann Peck. "Anna Hempstead Branch." *American Women Writers: A Critical Reference Guide from Colonial Times to the Present*. Edited by Lina Mainiero. New York: Frederick Ungar Publishing Co., 1979, 217–19.

Lane, Ann J. *To Herland and Beyond: The Life and Work of Charlotte Perkins Gilman.* New York: Pantheon Books, 1990.

Lehman, Eric. *Bridgeport: Tales from the Park City.* Charleston, SC: The History Press, 2009.

———. *Hamden: Tales from the Sleeping Giant.* Charleston, SC: The History Press, 2010.

L'Engle, Madeleine. *A Circle of Quiet.* New York: Farrar, Straus and Giroux, 1972.

———. *A Wrinkle in Time.* New York: Farrar, Straus and Giroux, 1962.

Lindbergh, Anne Morrow. *Gift from the Sea.* New York: Pantheon, 1955.

Lurie, Alison. *Familiar Spirits: A Memoir of James Merrill and David Jackson.* New York: Viking, 2001.

Marsden, George. *Jonathan Edwards: A Life.* New Haven, CT: Yale University Press, 2003.

Meredith, William. *Effort at Speech: New and Collected Poems.* Introduction by William Collier. New York: Triquarterly, 1997.

Merrill, James. *The Changing Light at Sandover.* Edited by J.D. McClatchy and Stephen Yenser. New York: Alfred A. Knopf, 2011.

———. *Collected Poems.* Edited by J.D. McClatchy and Stephen Yenser. New York: Alfred A. Knopf, 2001.

———. Interview with J.D. McClatchy. "The Art of Poetry No. 31." *Paris Review* 84 (1982). http://www.theparisreview.org.

Merrill, James, to Stephen Yenser. Letter. May 26, 1969. Reprinted in *Poetry* (Summer 1995): 324.

Miller, Arthur. *Collected Plays, 1944–1961.* New York: Library of America, 2006.

———. *Timebends: A Life.* New York: Grove Press, 1987.

Moers, Ellen. *Harriet Beecher Stowe and American Literature.* Hartford, CT: Stowe-Day Foundation, 1978.

Moran, Edward. "The Life and Poetry of Hyam Plutzik, 1911–1962." Hyam Plutzik Poetry. 2010. http://www.hyamplutzikpoetry.com.

Morgan, Bill. *Beat Atlas: A State by State Guide to the Beat Generation in America.* San Francisco: City Lights Books, 2011.

National Women's History Museum. "Emma Hart Willard." History of Women and Education. http://www.nwhm.org.

Nelson, Marilyn. *The Freedom Business: Including a Narrative of the Life & Adventure of Venture, a Native of Africa.* Honesdale, PA: Wordsong, 2008.

———. *How I Discovered Poetry.* New York: Penguin Group, 2014.

———. "A Literary History of Connecticut." Academy of American Poets. http://www.poets.org.

Niven, Penelope. *Thornton Wilder: A Life*. New York: HarperCollins, 2012.

O'Neill, Eugene. *A Long Day's Journey into Night*. New Haven: Yale University Press, 2002.

————. *Nine Plays*. New York: Modern Library, 1954.

Palm, Christine. "The Enigma of Wallace Stevens." *Hog River Journal* (Winter 2004–05). http://www.hogriver.org.

Poetry 11, no. 4 (January 1968).

Poetry Foundation. http://www.poetryfoundation.org.

Powers, Ron. *Mark Twain: A Life*. New York: Free Press, 2005.

Richardson, Joan. *Wallace Stevens, a Biography: The Early Years, 1879–1923*. New York: Beech Tree Books, 1986.

————. *Wallace Stevens, a Biography: The Later Years, 1923–1955*. New York: Beech Tree Books, 1988.

Schaefer, Patricia M. "The Joshua Hempstead Diary: A Window into Colonial Connecticut." Connecticut History Online. Connecticut Humanities. http://connecticuthistory.org.

Serafin, Steven R., ed. *Encyclopedia of World Literature in the 20th Century*. Vol. 1. New York: St. James Press, 1998.

Sigourney, Lydia Howard. *Illustrated Poems*. N.p.: Carey and Hart, 1849.

————. *Scenes in My Native Lands*. Boston: James Munroe and Company, 1845.

Smith, Elihu Hubbard. *American Poems Selected and Original*. Litchfield, CT: Collier and Buel, 1793.

Smith, Martha. "Leo Connellan: I Write about People Who Struggle Just to Stay Alive." *Providence Journal*, February 5, 1995.

Smith, Venture. *A Narrative of the Life and Adventures of Venture, a Native of Africa, but Resident Above Sixty Years in the United States of America*. New London, CT: C. Holt, 1798. Also available in Africans in America. PBS Online. www.pbs.org.

Stevens, Wallace. *The Collected Poems of Wallace Stevens*. New York: Vintage Books, 1990.

————. *Opus Posthumous*. Edited by Milton J. Bates. New York: Vintage Books, 1990.

Stowe, Charles Edward. *The Life of Harriet Beecher Stowe*. 1889. Reprint, 10th ed., Project Gutenberg, 2004.

Stowe, Harriet Beecher. *Uncle Tom's Cabin*. Everyman's Library. Edited by Ernest Rhys. London: J.M. Dent & Sons Ltd., 1943.

Stowe, Lyman Beecher. *Saints and Sinners and Beechers*. Indianapolis: Bubbs-Merrill Co., 1934.

Trumbull, John. *The Poetical Works of John Trumbull*. Hartford, CT: Samuel Goodrich, 1820.

Twain, Mark. *Adventures of Huckleberry Finn*. New York: Washington Square Press, 1973.

———. *Autobiography of Mark Twain*. Vol. 1. Berkeley: University of California Press, 2010.

———. *A Connecticut Yankee in King Arthur's Court*. New York: Harper and Brothers, 1917.

Warfel, Harry, ed. *Letters of Noah Webster*. New York: Library Publishers, 1953.

West, James L.W., II. *William Styron: A Life*. New York: Random House, 1998.

Wilder, Thornton. *The Bridge of San Luis Rey*. New York: HarperPerennial, 2003.

———. *Collected Plays and Writings on Theater*. Edited by J.D. McClatchy. New York: Library of America, 2007.

Zagarell, Sandra A. "Lydia Howard Sigourney." In *Heath Anthology of American Literature*. 5th ed. Edited by Paul Lauter. N.p.: Cengage Learning, 2012. Available online at http://college.cengage.com.

Index

INDEX

About the Authors

Eric D. Lehman and Amy Nawrocki are the co-authors of *A History of Connecticut Food* and *A History of Connecticut Wine*. Eric's essays, reviews and stories have appeared in dozens of journals and magazines, and his many books include *Becoming Tom Thumb: Charles Stratton, P.T. Barnum and the Dawn of American Celebrity, Afoot in Connecticut* and *The Insider's Guide to Connecticut*. Amy is an award-winning poet with three chapbooks, *Potato Eaters, Nomad's End* and *Lune de Miel*, as well as the full-length collection *Four Blue Eggs*. They teach English and creative writing at the University of Bridgeport and live in Hamden with their two cats.